Jesus: A Would Be King

BY

DR. HAROLD E. LITTLETON, JR., PH.D.

ISBN: 1439285772
ISBN 13: 9781439285770

Table of Contents

Introduction

"Very God of Very God," "made man."

For almost seventeen centuries the Christian church has wrestled with how to understand the nature of Jesus. Shaped by a pre-modern, pre-scientific world view, the followers of the apocalyptic, messianic prophet from Nazareth soon found themselves embroiled in a heated debate over what to believe and how to proclaim just who and what Jesus was. Some insisted, in traditional Jewish terms, that the messiah (moshiach) was to be a human being with historically realized goals on behalf of the Jewish people. Others quickly defined him as a spiritual entity, sent into our world to deliver the necessary "gnosis" for human salvation, but void of any genuine human, physical characteristics. This meant technically that he was unable to feel human desire or physically suffer. The interpretation that came to be "orthodox" and was embodied in the Nicene Creed was a hybrid compromise, politically motivated, that was not entirely acceptable to either extreme. There is much to be explored in the positions briefly described, but that is not the purpose of this book.

The expectations of the first group, known as Jewish or Ebionite Christians in contemporary parlance, were not fulfilled. The dualistic, otherworldly position, known as docetic or gnostic, must be rejected as a relic of pre-Enlightenment mentality. The synthesis found in the third resolution is rationally, philosophically, and theologically defenseless. However, over two billion believers today accept the explanation as "mystery" and move forward "on faith."

Unfortunately, in the process and in reality, for the overwhelming majority of Christians, any discussion or emphasis of the truly human nature of Jesus is offensive and ignored. Can you imagine Jesus performing bodily functions? Can you imagine Jesus having sex or fathering a child? I not only recognize that he could have but that he probably did, and I hope this is enough to entice you to enter the world I explore in the following pages.

This book is the product of an ongoing process covering forty years of study, research, conversation, and honest effort to go where the path led. I must thank former theology classmates, challenging professors, questioning colleagues, hundreds of students demanding that theses be defended, and fellow seekers, some willing and others reluctant, who encouraged this small effort to move the dialogue along.

I especially express gratitude to my daughters whose questions then and now force me to be open and humble. To my wife whose presence on this journey was and is indispensable, I am forever indebted.

A special word of gratitude to Dan Rosenthal for superior technological assistance.

- Harold E. Littleton, Jr., Ph.D.

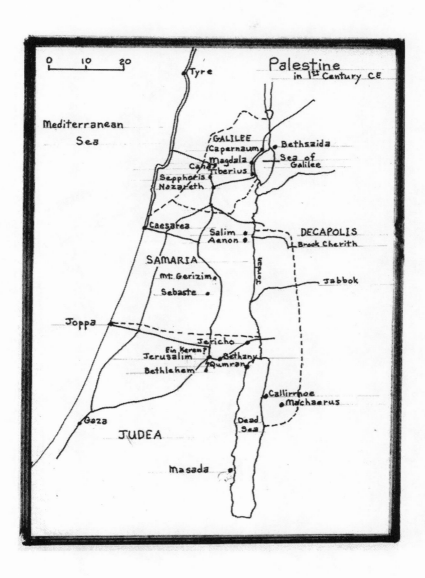

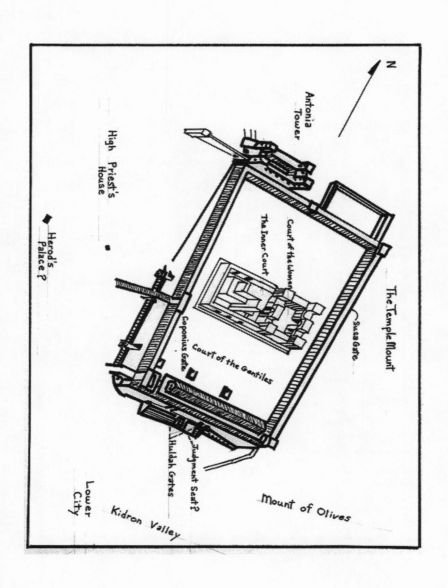

N

Antonia
Tower

High Priest's
House

Herod's
Palace ?

The Inner Court

Court of the Women

Susa Gate

The Temple Mount

Court of the Gentiles

Coponius Gate

Huldah Gates

Judgment Seat ?

Kidron Valley

Lower
City

Mount of Olives

SECTION I:

Caiaphas

CHAPTER 1

Looking back in retrospect

If I had known then what I know now, I would have let the little mamzer drown.

I love the seaside especially in early summer before it gets too hot and unpleasant. The cool breezes coming off the Sea of Galilee with the smells of fish and market help you forget. Even then I couldn't wait to get out of Jerusalem and head north. Despite the extra miles required to avoid the stinking, unclean Samaritans by detouring through the Decapolis, I didn't dread the five day trip. There was much to see, and playful games with children's mischievous antics helped pass the time quickly.

Our ancestral home in Capernaum was a needed get away. I never tired of hearing the stories. My patriarch Levi had asked Father Israel for a homestead as a family retreat in what the Romans called Galilee. He had agreed, and Levi settled on the northwest coast of the Sea. Fishing was bountiful and pasture lands were lush. Even though many relatives made the sojourn during the great drought, a few stayed, never relinquishing our claim to the land. When the Law Giver brought them home and Yeshua claimed the land, my ancestors were allowed to keep the small parcel for family use.

Being from the tribe of Levi it was our blessing and calling to serve the children of Abraham as perpetual priests. Serving the people and being served by the people put us in a unique position. We did not share in the distribution and assignment of the land like the other tribes. Especially when moshiach David conquered Jerusalem and centered the worship of the one true G-d in his new capitol, my family gathered there to perform our priestly duties. I have to admit it was a privileged life.

The rotation of Temple duties required proximity to the Temple Mount, and from the beginning, the choicest land was reserved for priestly families. While the Temple tax provided for the upkeep of the sanctuary, priestly vestments and implements (one robe correctly stitched and ornately embroidered could cost 500 denarii), and, except for the brief time following Yehudah Maccabeus' grand liberation, tribute to ruling overlords, it provided a very comfortable living for all the priestly families.

Grandfather Seth built the family compound in the fifth year of Pompey's rule. Jealousy and political intrigue pitted brother against brother and cousin against cousin. Pompey's enforced order brought an uneasy peace and, even if from external origins, much desired security. With that security, an important part of which was financial, Abba Annas' position was guaranteed. As High Priest it was imperative that he look and live the part. This included the finest of residential standards and a lifestyle that was the envy of everyone.

Abba Annas chose a promontory northwest of the Herodian Temple as the place to build his house. From here one had an unrestricted view of the gleaming walls and magnificent roof of the Temple. Direct access to the southwest stairs leading to the Coponius Gate let us observe all who came and went. He knew everything that happened, but more importantly, all who came and went could not avoid seeing our home and knowing that this was where the most important person in Jerusalem lived. Everyone, man, woman, child, Gentile, and Adonai's chosen people entered the Temple under the critical judgment and generous permission of the High Priest. Everyone answered to him. He answered to no one but G-d and of course Caesar.

Annas spared no expense. Despite jealousy and rumors of Temple treasury used for personal gain, the people of Israel had to understand that Adonai's priests deserved comfort in recompense for lives devoted to ritual performance. And his house had every comfort imaginable.

Built on three levels, it measured over 2000 square feet. The courtyard where guests first entered, household commerce was transacted, and
servants' and family pets were quartered opened to the west. On opposite
sides of this never quiet center of activity were two mikvot, one for males-
-the crown of Adonai's creation--and one for females, our given helpmates.
Every precaution was taken to guarantee personal, ritual purity, our obligation and gratitude to the one true G-d. The entire area was walled and
gated for necessary safety.

The second level contained the great Judgment Hall. Here Annas con-
ducted legal and civic business. One side opened to overlook the courtyard. From below family and interested parties to the discussions above saw
and heard as arguments were made and decisions rendered. On this level
the opulence was obvious and intentional. Mosaic floors done by the best
craftsmen in Jerusalem were everywhere. Breathtaking frescoes of elabo-
rate floral design covered every wall. The finest glassware and ceramics
the Mediterranean world had to offer were conspicuously placed throughout the Judgment Hall and adjacent banquet room. Carpets from Persia,
couches and tables intricately handcrafted from the mountains of Lebanon,
bronze and gold vessels from Egypt filled every space. The balcony that ran
the full length of the eastern side of the house provided the unobstructed
view of the Temple. Everyday the family could stand in awe of the gold
plated House of the L--d, established by Solomon and crowned by Herod.
The third level gave no less testimony to the prominence of this family.
It contained the private quarters where once again the creature comforts
lauded social status. From furniture to imported cosmetics, jewelry to silk
robes, crafted leather to Aegean purple, only Herod the Great himself could
boast of greater wealth.

Some people just could not understand or appreciate that rank has
privileges and responsibilities. Annas bore the heavy obligation of balanc-
ing Roman expectations and Temple requirements. Most critics were open,
sometimes violent, in their self-righteous opposition to ritual and monetary
levies; they could be controlled by Rome when necessary or more routinely
by Temple Guard. Other critics, even the handful among the priesthood,
were more subtle and passive in their protests.

For example, there was a minor functionary named Zechariah who deliberately chose to live outside the Temple compound and refused the financial support due his station. He took his wife, I think her name was

Elizabeth, to reside in Ein Kerem, rejecting the comforts of Jerusalem. Even when in late life they had a son, he stubbornly refused to bring them into the city. I unfortunately underestimated the depth of public support these voices controlled.

While my family never attained the office of High Priest itself, in important secondary roles we were responsible for the upkeep and cleanliness of the Temple proper, provided choir masters, served as musicians, and controlled security to the Temple Mount. As Chief Warden I got to know and be known by Annas, one of the most powerful and politically skillful men ever to serve as High Priest. Chosen to be his personal assistant, I developed religious and palace connections that proved to be very beneficial one day. It did not hinder those ambitions when I met Sarai, Annas' daughter, and we eventually married. Truth be told, I was closer to him than his blood sons and received his endorsement to become High Priest even before four of them.

Sarai and I built our house just north of her father's. The physical closeness allowed us to remain intimately involved in family activities. It also enabled me to maintain daily involvement with Annas, further learning religious and political skills that one day came in very handy and gave me access to his wisdom and judgment.

I had no idea how all of this would collide with the world of a Galilean peasant and change the course of my world.

CHAPTER 2

Summer in Capernaum

Before that marriage and the assumption of political and professional responsibilities, not to mention sadness and tragedy, came childhood innocence and summers of endless adolescent freedom. Capernaum was the center of my universe.

Between my 12th and 17th years father would take us north immediately after the celebration of Shavuot. [The rebellion of Yehudah the Galilean and the appointment of Annas to High Priest prevented our return after these years.] Having once again given thanks for deliverance from the hand of Pharoah and joyfully remembered Adonai's gift of the Law at Sinai, we longed for the quiet rest waiting for us by the Sea of Galilee. Our family custom was to stay here until after Sukkoth before returning to Jerusalem for Yom Kippur. While the differences between us and our distant peasant relatives were obvious, we nevertheless let our hair down, were a little more informal, relaxed and enjoyed a less demanding social observance as long as ritual purity was not violated. Father insisted on two mikvot in our house.

I think it was the summer of my 13th or 14th year that I first saw him. Even as a child of 6 or 7 he was different, unique, in a way hard to put in words. Oh, he was normal and mischievous. I remember being astonished by his sense of humor and the ease with which he related to adults and children alike. More astonishing was his relationship with men and women, as if he had no concept of limits or boundaries. And to the horror of my parents, he touched them all, tenderly and thoughtlessly.

We had not been in Capernaum a week, having left Jerusalem the day after Shavuot festival ended, and I could not contain my eagerness to swim and sail. The Sea was more beautiful than I remembered. The winter had been especially harsh with more snow than anyone recalled. In the distance the peaks of the Lebanon range glistened with the last, remaining drifts. As if it knew how precious and privileged its short life was, this pure blanket did not want to let go. Our hearts were torn between getting lost in their beauty and anticipating the rebirth of wheat fields, olive groves, and bountiful fish harvests. It was a time of fever-pitched activity as economic security depended on the success of these precious few months.

That particular morning I swallowed whole my breakfast of eggs, milk, cheese and dashed for the door.

"Caiaphas, you know I don't like for you to go to the water alone. It makes me nervous and I fear for your safety," Mother said as I almost escaped.

"Mother, I'll be fine. I know how to swim and, besides, there are plenty of people around."

"But." Too late. I was down the hill, out of sight and out of range.

By the time I reached the shore few boats remained beached. A hand full of fishermen, mostly boys, sat mending their nets. Heavy hauls take a toll on the nets and constant repairs are required if they are to be efficient.

I was always fascinated by the simple boats. If I hadn't been born to the station and destiny I was, I would have been a fisherman. Every chance I got I climbed aboard and enjoyed the wind in my face and sea spray soaking me from head to toe.

The boats were constructed efficiently for two reasons. Cost dictated that wood be reused when possible, new when necessary. Size was dictated by the available number of men to buy and build and the labor market available to do the fishing. Average size was 25 to 30 feet long and 10 feet wide, wide enough for two men to work side by side on opposite sides of the boat. There was a mast and a square sail that could be hoisted when getting to or returning from chosen locations. For those occasional times, and it was always frustrating when they came, when the sea was calm and no winds stirred, there were two sets of oars and a rudder to guide them home. To a young boy even rowing was a game and I often begged for the "privilege" of manning one of the oars. It took a while for me to realize why they smiled and so quickly allowed me to take a seat.

There was nothing like it in Jerusalem. It held no interest for my father. Maybe that is why he never seemed to understand my interest or the draw the water and boats had on me. G-d loved it too.

וְרוּחַ אֱלֹהִים, מְרַחֶפֶת עַל-פְּנֵי הַמָּיִם

"and the spirit of the G-d was moving over the face of the waters." I love Jerusalem and I love the Temple, but here, beside the Sea, I feel oneness with Adonai and become one with His creation.

You can swim and skip rocks and carry fish in baskets only so long before tiring. Breakfast was long forgotten and the mid-day sun stole my energy. I was hungry and getting a little sleepy.

I noticed him but paid little interest this particular morning. Along with his younger brother he played and swam near where I had been most of the day. Apparently, despite being warned not to, he swam to a boat anchored about thirty feet from shore. He climbed into the boat and dove off the gunnels several times. But this time he didn't come up like usual.

Perhaps he was playing a trick on his brother and hiding on the side of the boat opposite the shore. Perhaps little brothers are insecure when in a crowd of unfamiliar faces. For whatever reason, the young one was not in the mood to be tricked. He began to scream, "Yeshua, Yeshua." I don't know why, but the tone of his plaintive cry caught my attention.

"He won't come up! He won't come up! Help!"

I grabbed his arm and demanded to know where he had seen him last. All the boy could do was point at the boat. The men nearby either thought it was a joke or paid no attention, too busy to be involved in child's play.

Without thinking, I was in the water before realizing what I was doing. Later they said I swam to the boat and, once I crawled into the boat and stood searching the crystal clear water on either side, dove over the stern. I would remember a lifeless form on the bottom, ten feet down. After grasping an arm, I pulled him to the surface. My lungs burned as if on fire like the pit of Gehenna. Thanks be to G-d we came up right beside the boat and I was able to reach a gunnel while holding him with my other hand.

By this time a couple of the fishermen realized what was happening. They made it to the boat just as we broke the surface. They quickly took him and together got him to the shore. One of the men, tanned and weathered from years of hard labor with the Sea, picked him up as if he were a twig. Doing the only thing he knew to do or had done who knows how many times before, he pulled him to his naked body, wrapped his burly arms around his chest, and rhythmically squeezed and released his boyish frame. By now I was back on shore and, standing with my arm around his brother, did the only thing I could now—watched and prayed.

It seemed like an eternity, but suddenly and slowly he gasped. Out spewed water and vomit. The man held him upright as he wretched and heaved and fought for the tiniest amount of air he could get. And once he could breathe on his own, the man just held him until his labored respiration calmed, his crying stopped, and he understood what had happened. United, the brothers stood entwined in one another's arms silently sobbing.

Not wishing to intrude in something so personal, I quietly gathered my robe and sandals and started for the house. Before I reached the path that would take me up the hill home, I heard running steps behind me and a voice calling, "Wait."

It was he. Once he got within five feet of me he stopped.

"I am Yeshua, Yeshua bar Yehosef. What is your name?"

"I am Yosef Caiaphas."

"You saved my life. I have nothing to give you except my friendship. If I can ever save you, I will."

"Don't be silly. What can you, one of the am ha 'aretz do for me? I am from the house of Levi."

"I'm from the house of David but we can be friends. This is my brother Yaaqov. He said you were very brave, swimming to get me. Maybe we'll see you tomorrow. We go back to Nazareth before Shabbat."

"Maybe. If you're not from Capernaum, why are you here anyway?"

"My father had some business here and we're staying with my uncle Clophas. Do you know him?"

"No, but we live in Jerusalem and only come up here during the summer for rest. My father serves in the Temple. Well, I've got to go."

"Shalom."

"Shalom."

*　*　*

CHAPTER 3

Accommodation and conflict

I cannot say that things have always been peaceful and quiet in Judea. Some would say we haven't had peace since the reign of David. Well, there was that interlude with the Hasmoneans. I would argue that Herod the Great did more to reestablish the grandeur of Israel than anyone in memory. He truly delivered us from the oppression of the Romans, secured freedom, and with the restoration of the Temple beyond anything imagined by Solomon, purified the worship of Adonai once again in Jerusalem. Unfortunately, he died.

Combined, his three sons weren't half the man or king Herod was. Malcontents, bandits, and ignorant rabble did not appreciate life as we enjoyed it under Herod. Their violent, rebellious acts following his death were not going to be tolerated by the Romans. Subsequently the kingdom was divided.

Change is never easy, even in the best of times. When you live on the edge and everyday is a challenge just to survive, people are susceptible to the promises of the most ignorant reprobates. Galilee had long been a hotbed for unrest and political instability. All they needed was the least provocation, and Herod's death provided the occasion.

Personally I can't say I totally disapproved. I do understand that when the Roman overlords required 25% of all agricultural production—it takes a lot to feed and maintain such a massive military machine and the administrative behemoth in Rome—and Jerusalem requires the annual shekel for Temple and priests, people are not left much to care for and feed themselves. On top of that rent must be paid to the overlords. Those people should have been more frugal and not fallen into such debt.

When someone like Yehudah bar Ezekias comes along and tells them not to pay their taxes, their debts are forgiven, and they are the rightful owners of the land, rebellion and freedom hold more promise than continuing in their squalid existence. Publius Quintilius Varus wasted no time in sending the 6th Legion into Galilee, burning Sepphoris, and massacring thousands.

Herod Antipas' restoration of Sepphoris was briefly interrupted by another false messiah's claims and armed insurrection. Perhaps Galilee's reputation as the refuge for the Davidic family after the destruction of the Temple at the hands of the Babylonians, perhaps the village of Kokhaba's claim to be the "star" from which the moshiach would arise and re-establish the greatness of Israel, perhaps it was Nazareth's claim to be the home of the stomp of Jesse's branches, it doesn't matter. They were misguided and chose to turn their backs on Zion.

We knew how to co-exist. The hope of Israel, G-d's chosen, rests with us, the Sadducees. We know the Torah; we preserve the house of YHWH; we know what is required: purity, loyalty, sacrifice, obedience.

Whatever the cause, Yehudah the Galilean's view of history was shortsighted. Like his predecessor and his successors, his revolt was doomed from the beginning. Father refused to take us to Capernaum that year. "It is not safe for your mother and sisters," he declared. When I heard the news that the Romans had crucified Yehudah along with over two thousand of his followers, I reluctantly admitted he was right.

Galilee is over sixty miles from Jerusalem and history taught us that even the city of David is not immune to violence. While the revolt lasted we listened for reports with fear and anticipation. We were caught in the middle between a mad Galilean and a mad descendant of Herod. Our loyalty was to YHWH and preserving His house and city. I can't imagine what the death and destruction must have been like for an eleven year old boy from Nazareth. I heard his father was caught up in the chaos and either innocently killed by the rebels or executed by Varus.

The years that Seth served Herod and the strong personal ties nurtured by Annas with Herod and his sons positioned us well for the coming uncertainty. Archelaus was insensitive and incompetent. He wouldn't last barely ten years. Philip was weak and indecisive. Fortunately I had known Herod Antipas since I was a child. We shared the same hopes and visions for this land. We respected each other's strengths and supported each other's weaknesses. We would find ourselves one day cooperating to save our nation and faith from unimaginable blasphemy.

Archelaus never understood the relationship between king and high priest. So when Herod died, he arrogantly ignored Seth, even to the point of public humiliation. For the sake of the nation Seth tolerated the abuse but worked diligently behind the scenes to position Annas for the day when Archelaus would be replaced. It was inevitable given his self-centered opulence supported by increased taxes and further hardships placed on the people.

When political and economic conditions were no longer tolerable, to Judeans or Romans, Quirinius' heavy hand squashed him like a fly and shipped him off to exile in Gaul. Quirinius was not a Jew lover, but he had been given an assignment, knew the long standing relationship between Rome and Jerusalem, and intended to make the best of a tenuous circumstance. To that end and with no small amount of encouragement from Herod Antipas, he appointed Annas High Priest immediately after securing the city of David.

We have always been good at political deception. Annas was a master. While Quirinius assumed outer control, Annas deepened the priesthood's control of Temple, treasury, and people's loyalty. We hated the Romans and dreamed of freedom. Even when Valerius Gratus succeeded Quirinius and sought to put his own stamp on the face of Judea by dismissing Annas, Annas' power was not reduced in the least.

Valerius Gratus shortly learned that his will and goals went nowhere without Annas' approval. The quick succession of Ishmael bar Phabi, Eleazer, and Shimon bar Camithus as high priests yielded nothing but turmoil for the Romans. Finally, with Annas' strong persuasion in face of mounting unrest, Valerius Gratus appointed me as High Priest four years after the death of Augustus.

Before the unrest, the dismissal of Annas, and my eventual succession to the office of High Priest, and after the swimming accident and first encounter with Yeshua bar Yosef, there were enjoyable, bucolic summers spent in Capernaum. Solomon had built the house of YHWH on what we lovingly call the Temple Mount. There is no place like it on earth, and there is no substitute for it. However, villages at great distances from Jerusalem were beginning to build small structures for civic meetings and specifically for the "synagogue" to meet on Shabbat for worship and the reading of the Law. With reticence and after an extended lecture on its secondary importance, Father even contributed to the construction of such a building in Capernaum.

I never saw it completed, but as children we watched the craftsmen at their trade and played among the rising walls and supporting columns. It appeared to be about 40 feet by 90 feet. I even heard talk of something called the seat of Moses where the weekly reader would sit with the unrolled scroll to discuss the Shabbat portion.

To be truthful I had practically forgotten the incident at the Sea that morning. But about a week later, when I was back swimming and asking every question I could think of about fishing, there he was again.

"Caiaphas! Caiaphas!"

"Oh, shalom."

"Shalom. Want to go swimming?" he inquired.

"Don't you think you've had enough for one summer?"

"I'm sorry I scared you, but I'm awfully glad you were there. I promise to be more careful."

"Where is your brother?"

"He wanted to come but Mother kept him with her this morning."

After a couple of hours swimming and playing in the sun, breakfast was forgotten and we both were hungry. Not to be impolite, and knowing that he and his people were simple peasants, I invited him home for mid-day meal.

"We're starving and I have a friend with me," I said as we entered the courtyard.

Mother was sitting in the shade sewing a scarf for my sister. Looking up somewhat startled, all she could say was "Oh, well wash yourselves before you come in." We quickly stepped into the mikveh, washed our hands and faces, and met her at the table.

I knew he could not be used to even these modest surroundings, but he did not seem threatened or impressed. Rather he was quite comfortable. My mother watched him cautiously as we ate the bread, dried fish, and olives and drank the cool water, afraid that he would break something. She had to acknowledge, after he left, that he was well-mannered, even casually at home and in control.

"Thank you very much. I need to get home. Father asked me to help him with something this afternoon. Anyway we are going home to Nazareth tomorrow. Will you come back to Capernaum?"

"We'll be back next year after Shavuot."

"Maybe I'll see you then."

"Shalom."

"Shalom."

I didn't see him again the rest of that summer. Either the family didn't return to Capernaum or we never found our way to the sea shore at the same time. Maybe his father's work kept them in Nazareth. Who knows? Who cares? I forgot about him anyway.

But the next summer, within two weeks of our return, there he was, swimming and talking with the fishermen.

"Shalom. Caiaphas!"

"Shalom."

"It's me, Yeshua, last year, you saved my life."

"Oh, yeh."

"Where have you been? What have you been doing?

"We went back to Jerusalem after Sukkoth and only got back two weeks ago. I told you my father serves in the Temple. What have you been doing? Can you swim any better this year?"

"You won't let me forget, will you?" he said with a smile. There was no embarrassment on his face. "I have so much to tell you. I've seen so much and learned so much. Abba Yosef lets me help him digging foundations, and carrying the rocks for the walls, and I got to go with him to Sepphoris, and...."

"Wait! Slow down. You don't have to tell me everything today."

"You're right. I'm sorry. I didn't give you a chance to tell me about your year. Tell me about Zion. We haven't been able to go since the king's death. It must be beautiful. Do the walls touch the sky? Is the Temple really built out of gold? Do the Romans really make you eat pigs? Mother says I have a cousin there, but I've never seen him."

"One at a time, please! It's a long way and I'm glad we don't do it more than once a year. And yes, Jerusalem is the most beautiful city in the world. David must have been the greatest king ever for G-d to give him such a place. You can see the Temple shining in the sun for a whole day before you get there. The walls are the strongest and the tallest you will ever see. And the Temple is more beautiful than I can describe. It is G-d's house. I would die to protect it. King Herod was the greatest builder of all time and every Jew should be proud. And no, the Romans don't make us eat pigs!"

"Now your turn," said Caiaphas, catching his breath while thinking, "I'm older and deserve some respect from this little peasant."

"Well after that, I hardly have anything to say."

"Of course you do. Living here can't be all bad."

"When we went back to Nazareth last year, I told Mother all about your house and your family. She let me carry on forever and then she reminded me that the greatest treasure we have is G-d's love. Our house is simple, mud and stone and straw, but I can sleep on the roof when it's warm and own countless stars, and when it's cold, I can sleep with the sheep to stay warm. We don't have the fine clothes or beautiful furniture you have, but we have the flowers, the mountains on the horizon, and Father Noah's rainbow."

"You're weird," I said but couldn't help thinking how enviably simple his life was.

"Race you to the boat!"

We played, swam, and explored Capernaum the rest of that week. Capernaum wasn't and isn't that big so we learned our way around quickly. Our parents weren't worried about us since everyone seemed to know everyone. His little brother Yaaqov tagged along some days. Yeshua said his father was helping his uncle build a house for a Roman official that had recently moved to town.

"What's Sepphoris like? I knew Herod Antipas in Jerusalem before his father died. I hear he plans to make it the capitol of Galilee but it'll never be as beautiful as Jerusalem. He'll never be the king his father was."

"I don't know about all that. It's not much right now. Abba works there, every week. It's only a short walk from home. Anyway our ancestors were kings but my real king is YHWH."

"You're stupid! If you talk like that you're going to get in trouble."

We continued to argue and call one another names until we both got so angry we stomped off home saying we hoped never to see one another again.

CHAPTER 4

New families, new love

After a couple of years when Father thought it safe again to travel to Capernaum, he and I returned to Galilee. I could hardly believe my eyes. The destruction was overwhelming, villages burned and left without repair, farms neglected, untilled, unplanted, people malnourished, wearing rags. We got reports that our house had suffered a fire and the outer wall to the courtyard leveled. Forewarned, we weren't prepared for what we saw.

Father sent word for the servants to prepare for our arrival as best they could. He was anxious to see for himself and to oversee personally any restoration if there was to be any.

Any enthusiasm he had visibly disappeared the minute the house came into sight. The servants had been able to clear two rooms so we had a roof over our heads. The courtyard was cluttered beyond use, and the mikvah was filled with dirt and stones. If Father had not remembered where it was situated, no one would have had the slightest idea where to look. Given purity requirements, clearing and filling the mikvah with living water was the first priority.

These ignorant Galileans cannot be trusted to do anything. Other than the minimal clean up they had done, knowing of our imminent arrival, the servants seemed to loathe our presence and took no initiative to make our visit comfortable.

When I realized that my father was at a loss as to where to begin, I stepped in to ask if anyone knew a tekton who might be available to work on our house at least a month or two while we assessed the damage and decided whether or not to rebuild. Nathan, who had served the family since I was an infant, said he thought a man by the name of Clophas might be available. Since he lived in lower Capernaum, on the road to Magdala, Nathan offered to contact him.

With nothing to do but wait, we made a make shift bed in each corner of one room, set a table in the middle for a lantern, and began clearing the other room for a table and reclining couches. Nathan's wife Sarai offered to prepare a meager meal for the evening. Nathan returned before sunset and said Clophas would come by the next morning.

Gratefully it didn't rain. With two holes in the roof, I can't imagine getting much sleep with only a wet cloak for cover. Sarai managed to gather enough fruits and left over bread to curb our hunger.

After evening prayers, which I recited because Father was still too dazed and overwhelmed to take charge, we settled down for a restless night.

"Shema Israel..."

Imagine my surprise about mid-morning when Clophas arrived at our house. With him was this young boy, now 13 or 14, but immediately recognized. It was Yeshua!

"Yeshua! What are you doing here? How do you know this man?"

He was as startled as I was and rushed to grab my arm.

"Nathan didn't say it was your house, but when he described the location and said the owner hadn't been here since before the revolt, I hoped it was you. It's been so long—what, three or four years since you were here? So much has happened. Where are your mother and your sister?"

"When reports of the war reached Jerusalem and Father heard the house had been damaged, he thought it better to wait to return until he was sure it was safe. You can see the women would not be comfortable. They're not used to doing too much work. But you didn't tell me why you are in Capernaum and how you know this man?"

I asked Father if he needed me in the conversation with Clophas. He indicated not for now, and after I told him how I knew Yeshua, he and I set off to catch up on all the missing years.

Despite the difference in our ages, he was amazingly easy to talk with. I was impressed with his knowledge of everything that had happened, but more impressed with his strong opinions. Most boys in Jerusalem were too busy playing games and chasing girls to have political opinions. Then I reminded myself, he had lived what happened here, not just heard about it from a safe, protected distance.

"You still haven't told me what you are doing here and how you know this man."

"You know we lived in Nazareth. It was a small village, smaller now since the Romans came through. My father worked in Sepphoris but wanted Mother and my brother and me safe and away from the dangers of a bigger city. When Yehudah the Galilean rose up to claim our rightful freedom and tried to return the land to the true Israel, my father was so excited. He told me one day I would grow up to lead the new Israel, as a descendent of David. It is my birthright."

"You're crazy in the head!"

"Well, sometimes I wonder. Anyway, you know, the Romans defeated Yehudah and their anger knew no limits. My father, Yosef, was killed trying to defend Sepphoris. I guess we're lucky. They didn't know who he was so they didn't come looking for us. Mother took Yaaqov and me into the hill country and hid us until the troops quit burning and killing everything they saw. We didn't even get to bury my father. When she thought she could get here without getting caught, we walked at night and hid during the day. It's not that far but it took a week to get here. Clophas is my uncle and now he is my father. He told me something about Moses and Levite law. Anyway, he's a good man and provides for us well."

"You are lucky to be alive and you don't have any idea what you're talking about. Yehudah was a stupid, ignorant zealot. Any future we have as a nation rests in the hands of the priests, the Temple, and cooperation with Rome. They are too big, too powerful, and too brutal to resist. You stupid peasants have got to learn to listen to us in Jerusalem who have figured out what it takes to survive."

"You and I aren't going to settle this today. One day I hope you will remember G_d gave this land to Father Abraham and called us to be a blessing to all nations. G_d is our king and we are supposed to live by His rules, not some foreigner's."

"If you want to live, you will live by their rules!"

"Caiaphas, it's been too long. Let's not argue today. We'll have time to work this out. Right now I'm glad you're back and I'm glad I can help rebuild your house."

By the time Yeshua and I returned Father and Clophas had struck a deal and fortunately he was free to start the repairs the next day. They left to return home and we spent the rest of the day trying to make our quarters as comfortable as possible for the time we would stay.

True to his word Clophas showed up early with his meager tools and Yeshua by his side. Yeshua was big enough now to be of help to his uncle/ father, so he and I had little time for conversation or idle walks. I shouldn't have been surprised, but he hadn't said a word about it. About midday a woman showed up carrying a small child and visibly expecting another. She turned out to be his mother and had brought them the food they had forgotten in their haste to get started early.

"This is my mother, Maria, and this is my brother, Yaaqov bar Alpheus (Clophas)."

"Shalom."

"Shalom. My son has told me so much about you. You are kind to take up your time with a younger boy."

"Oh, it's no problem and, besides, there aren't that many boys around here, my age or younger. Don't you have another son?"

"Yes, but he wasn't feeling well. So I let him stay home. Well I need to get back and check on him. I'm sorry about your house but glad you hired my husband and son. Shalom."

She seemed warm and genuine, unlike many of the self-centered, gossipy women I know in Jerusalem. But I couldn't help feeling sorry for her. She had her hands full with three sons and expecting another child. Life is a challenge in Galilee, anyway you look at it.

Given their schedule and the fact that Yeshua really was needed in assisting Clophas, we rarely said two words to each other for the next two months. Father continued my instruction for the priestly duties I would assume upon returning to Zion and, unbelievably, the synagogue in Capernaum had a Torah scroll. I was able to spend many hours lost in the wonder of G-d's word given to Moses, pondering the mystery of this gift.

And then there was Sarai to think about. For some time now it had been decided. Father had long conversations with Annas. This marriage would unite my family with the most important priestly family in Jerusalem, a marriage of mutual economic benefit, shared religious viewpoints and **and** undeniable political goals. I would marry her no matter what. But in the bargain I got the most beautiful young woman I had ever seen until......

Until the day before we were to leave Capernaum and begin the journey home. The work went well. Quite frankly I thought the house looked grander than before the revolt. Walls were repaired. It was impossible to tell there had been holes in the thatched roof. All debris had been removed and the inside walls plastered. The artisan was contracted for the dining room fresco and completed the project before we were scheduled to return the following year. Father and I saw examples of Clophas' carpentry, and he would build a new dining table and couches.

Yeshua and I planned to spend the last afternoon saying our goodbyes. Thoughtlessly and aimlessly we meandered the entire length of the boulevard that ran north and south parallel to the shore, passed the gymnasium and the barracks. As we wandered among the boats and nets and fishmongers hawking their catches, we both saw her at the same time. She was young, couldn't have been more than Yeshua's age. His was an innocent and pure attraction. Mine was mature with an awareness of potential. Despite myself I blushed with guilt. I was pledged and had no right to entertain any thoughts of physical attraction. Her unblemished body was only beginning to reveal the blossoming figure of womanhood. Her hair shone in the radiant Galilean sun and her olive complexion was flawless. It was her midnight eyes, those almond, chocolate eyes that pierced my heart and I never forgot.

I am ashamed to admit that despite my age and social position, I was speechless. Not so Yeshua. Without hesitation he walked right up to her.

"I haven't seen you here before. Are you from Capernaum?"

"No, but we come often. My father is a merchant from Magdala. He lets me come with him when he brings the salted fish to sell to the Romans or caravans that come through here.

Their rapport was instant and naïve. I was jealous....and angry with myself for these unwanted feelings.

"My name is Yeshua."

"I'm Mariamne."

"Mariamne, get over here. How many times have I told you not to speak to strangers!"

"But Father..."

"But nothing. Come here."

In a minute it was over. But somehow I knew it wouldn't be the last time I would see her.

SECTION II:

Yeshua

CHAPTER 5

A Father's protection

I would see him once more before our final confrontation.

Caiaphas and his father left for Jerusalem the next day. I sensed some tension, an uneasiness, but couldn't quite put my finger on it. Abba Clophas and I continued with the work left to do. It was a good thing because our family grew by leaps and bounds in the coming years. After Yaaqov of Alphaeus there was Shimon who would be called the Zealot because of his hot temper, Matya of Alphaeus called Levi to honor Mother's grandfather and great-grandfather, Salome, a "gift" for my mother in a house full of males, Yosa named with affection for my father, Elizabeth to keep Salome company, and finally Yehudah of Alphaeus. For a while it seemed as if a baby was born before the last one could even walk.

In the midst of this loving chaos I was reminded everyday who I am and who my ancestors were. Mother treasured those names, and with Abba Yosef's death, she was the one who preserved that history and passed it to me. From an early age my royal and priestly roots were planted in my heart and head. Yosef and Maria "married" those traditions and I embodied them. Their literalness and their meaning never let me rest.

And while my name—Yeshua, deliverer—defined me, my brothers' names were equally significant.

"The blood of kings and priests <u>and</u> liberators runs in your veins," she told us. "Remember the great Mastitis (as she winked at Matya). With his sons they threw off the yoke of the Gentiles, cleansed the Temple, and restored the pure worship of the one true G-d: Yehudah the Hammer, Yonathan called Yoses, Shimon full of zeal for YHWH. Father Yaaqov lives in Yaaqov of Yehosef and Yaaqov of Clophas. Your destiny is in the 'stars.' You will restore the reign of G-d to his people."

Before I knew what it meant, my heart was captured by Mariamne. I thought about her every waking moment and dreamed of her every night. I went back to the fish market everyday, but she had vanished like frosted breath on a winter's morning.

It would be a year before my prayers were answered. There she was, with her father Yohanan, bargaining with the traders, and smiling coyly. She was an asset to her father, melting the hardened hearts of old men, and demolishing their greedy defenses. Remembering the last words I heard her father utter, I walked up to him and spoke to him directly.

"Shalom. I am Yeshua of Nazareth and live in Capernaum with my mother and Abba Clophas the builder. May I speak to your daughter?"

By now she remembered our first encounter but averted her eyes without revealing our knowledge of one another. Maybe it was my bravery, my respect for him, or my naivety, but he looked at me from head to toe for what seemed an eternity. Finally he responded. "You may tell her your name and leave. Don't come back without your father."

"I'm Yeshua." Just in case she had forgotten. I could tell from her smile she hadn't.

"I'm Mariamne." Without the slightest indication that I had ever heard it before. She had the voice of an angel.

"I'll be back."

I don't know what I was thinking. I wasn't thinking. A girl from Magdala with a merchant for a father. A boy from Capernaum learning a trade. I had to find Abba and bring him back. They could be gone tomorrow and I would never see her again.

"Abba, Abba. You must come with me." With gushing excitement I told him all of the little bit that had passed between us and begged him to come meet her father.

"You talk like you're trying to get me to arrange a marriage and you're only 14. There's plenty of time; we have work to do."

"Please Abba please!"

Urgency, persistency, or simply to get it behind us, he consented. I ran the whole way back, fearing they would have finished their transactions and left for who knows where.

To my joy they were still there although it looked like they were about to pack their belongings. I didn't wait for Clophas to catch up. Pointing to him as he approached, I blurted out, "That's my father."

"Shalom. I am Clophas of Capernaum. My son has asked that ....."

I quickly moved beside Mariamne and watched without hearing their stilted and then relaxed conversation. Clophas is a gentle man, easy to like and talk to. I did hear him say, "What harm can there be in two youths just talking. They aren't going anywhere and we are right here with careful eyes. It's not like we are arranging a marriage!" With a smile and nod of their heads, we knew it was alright.

Magdala, mother who died giving her birth, raised by her father's sister, no siblings, contrary to custom learning her father's business, never out of his sight. She knew it was for her own good. They came to Capernaum once a month between planting and harvest. They had been to Jerusalem for Pesah once, but she knew her father resented the ostentatious hypocracy of many of the priests. Like my family they remembered David and worshiped YHWH in reverence and humility.

All too soon the fathers ended our conversation, saying it was time to return home.

"We'll be back in two fortnights. Please come and look for me."

"I promise. Shalom."

Three more times before Sukkoth we met under the watchful and critical eyes of her father. We waded in the cool waters of the crystal clear sea and warmed our faces and hearts in the glorious Galilean sun. I don't have the words to express the closeness and depth of my feelings for her. There were other girls in Capernaum and Nazareth the time or two we had returned to visit relatives, but they had never been more than faceless images in the tapestry of the village. With Mariamne it was as if there had never been a time we didn't know each other. I opened my soul to her, and she to me. Even when I shared the intimacies of my forebearers and the dreams and mission of my deepest surrender to Adonai, she didn't ridicule me. Rather she accepted that future as her own and pledged to help in any way she could.

Youthful infatuation or genuine love, I really can't say. I only know it would be a long winter before seeing her again.

CHAPTER 6

Disappointment and widened rift

Following Pesah Abba Clophas and I began repairs on the house of widow Berenice. Along with her daughter Marta the widow provided for them by serving the family of the centurion quartered in Capernaum. They cooked, cleaned, and took care of his children.

Their house was close to the shore, situated on the main street that ran north/south the entire length of Capernaum. Actually it wasn't just her house. Berenice and Marta occupied two rooms that faced the open L-shaped courtyard shared by another family. The beam and thatched roof was old and, during the heavy snow two weeks after the Feast of Dedication, a corner portion had collapsed. We made a temporary patch to get them through until spring, and then we returned to do a more permanent repair.

Everyday I watched the fish market eagerly waiting for Mariamne to return. I knew she was fast approaching marriageable age. Families were generally anxious to get their daughters married, one less mouth to feed. I also knew I wasn't the best marriage prospect to her father. My only hope was that Clophas would convince her father that together, we could build an additional room on our house for her and me and that a budding apprentice would always find work to provide a relatively comfortable living. And that Mariamne could convince her father that this was her deepest wish and happiness.

I had long conversations with Mother and Clophas. Our compromise was that, while they still thought I was too young (Mother had birthed me by the age of Mariamne!), they agreed to propose betrothal to her father. They didn't offer much encouragement and reminded me that it was still his decision.

Always aware that anything could happen since their last trip north, I was quite relieved at last when I saw them at the market. Having earned the privilege of greeting them without my parents' presence, I spoke to Yohanan and respectfully asked permission to talk with Mariamne. Always close and under his scrutiny, we restrained ourselves from touching and shared our deepest affection in long, caressing stares. Honestly I couldn't take my eyes off her.

I had to get to Berenice's house; Clophas was waiting. But before leaving I asked Yohanan if he would be back the next day. I told him that my father wanted to speak with him. He gave me a questioning look but said they would be back. I smiled at Mariamne as I left for the day's work.

It is the father's responsibility to make decisions for the family and their children's welfare. But because Mother knew that her mother had died years before, she thought it was important that Yohanan meet her and know that, if he agreed, his daughter would become part of a loving and caring family guided by a capable mother.

So the next morning, before starting the day's work, Mother and Abba walked with me to find Yohanan and his daughter. True to his word, they were back. After the men greeted each other and went through the formalities of casual conversation, Clophas introduced Mother and told him a little more about our family and life in Capernaum.

My stomach was churning. I couldn't stand still, and Mariamne knew something important was taking place despite the fact that we had never used the word "marriage."

Yohanan seemed surprised. He uttered something about childhood friendship and at least pretended to be caught off guard. They moved a little farther down the shore from us and continued their conversation. Finally I saw Clophas and Yohanan shake hands, and they all moved back toward us.

"Come along Yeshua. We are late and there is much to do."

"But…"

"Come along."

Quietly and obediently, after stealing a glance at Mariamne, I fell in behind them and walked toward Berenice's house. I didn't know if I should sing or cry. Back up on the street and at last in front of the house, Abba said, "He didn't say 'no' but only agreed to think about it."

"Well, when will he decide?"

"I did not press him. He will decide when he decides, and he'll tell us then, not before."

"But…"

"Yeshua, that's the end of it now. Patience. It is in Adonai's hands."

Of course that argument was hard to challenge (it wouldn't be the last time my life would be in Adonai's hands) but my world seemed shattered. The rest of the day was a blur; it lasted forever and I don't remember a single thing we did.

Shabbat began at sunset so we did allow ourselves time to gather our tools and get home before the sun disappeared behind the hills. We bathed and gathered our tzitzits. Mother had prepared a simple but ample meal. Once we were seated she lit the candles and intoned the ancient prayer. Traditionally we males were served first and when I asked why she always ate after we did, she lovingly reminded me that Mother Eve was given as a helpmate to Abba Adam.

"It hardly seems fair. You work as hard as we do with responsibilities of caring for the children. Your work is precious in Adonai's eyes."

"It's not that my work is less important and I don't feel unappreciated. Adonai made Adam first and Eve came second."

"Adonai made them both. He made us all. We are all precious in His sight and loved equally."

Clophas sat quietly during this conversation.

It might have been my imagination or maybe Abba and I made some effort to be more helpful around the house, but Mother began eating and sharing meal time with us rather than later. Clophas and I took more time with the smaller children, feeding them and preparing them for bedtime. It was a relationship that felt right.

The next morning Clophas and I went to Shabbat assembly. I was caught off guard when Caiaphas and his father joined the crowd. It took some effort not to stand and shout and wave. So when service ended, I ran as fast as possible to greet them and welcome them back. Yohanan was also at service, but I noticed that he avoided speaking to these Jerusalem visitors. I would find out why soon enough.

Caiaphas and I quickly found a way to excuse ourselves and headed for the shore.

"Well my young friend, you'll never guess what's happened to me." And before I could even try he blurted out, "I'm married."

"You're kidding," I stuttered. "You never even mentioned anybody you cared about, much less might marry. Who? When? Where?"

"One question at a time. Her name is Sarai; she is the daughter of Annas, the High Priest. I've known who she is for sometime, but we had never spoken. Unknown to us our fathers had been talking about a marriage of the families for a couple of years. She's five years younger than I but our fathers thought it was time we both got married. Of course I'd obey my father; I understand the political advantages of having Annas for a father-in-law. But I am doubly blessed. She is beautiful, reverent, well-trained, and obedient. She'll be a good wife."

"I didn't hear you say you love her."

"That will come with time. Right now my career is what's important, and she can help see that I'll be respected and, who knows, maybe one day high priest myself."

"Being a priest is being a servant. I don't hear you talking very much about serving Adonai by serving the people. You seem a little hung up on what's in it for you. Sometimes I wonder about the Temple and all the money they get."

"Still the idealist you back water idiot! You had better open your eyes, Yeshua. It takes power to get anything done. And we have to survive while building that power. The Romans are a reality that won't go away soon. I know which side my bread has honey on. You can talk about Adonai's kingdom all you want but Adonai needs me to get His work done."

"I'm not so sure about all that Caiaphas, but I do know that if G-d doesn't rule in our hearts, it doesn't matter how rich or powerful we are. To rule the world without the love of G-d is a pretty empty and meaningless life."

"I can love G-d in Jerusalem, maybe better."

"G-d doesn't want your sacrifices and incense, Caiaphas. He wants justice, jubilee, and mercy. Jerusalem seems to have forgotten."

"You're impossible! I hope you grow up soon or at least learn to keep your mouth shut."

"Adonai doesn't want a priesthood; He wants a nation of priests. He doesn't want a house made of stones. He wants to dwell in our hearts. Love Adonai and love one another. Don't you get it?"

The conversation ended in a stalemate or, if possible, even worse than the last time we talked. I regretted his anger and the loss of friendship, but it was increasingly clear that Caiaphas had a different agenda for himself and for Israel.

"Wasn't that Caiaphas of Jerusalem and his father Yosef?" asked Yohanan as Caiaphas stormed up the beach and out of sight.

"Yes, but how do you know them?"

"I had to be in Jerusalem for business last winter during the Feast of Dedication. There was a huge wedding ceremony on the stairs of the Temple Mount. They even blocked entry to the inner courts while it was going on. I've never seen such pomp and arrogance. I thought I recognized the young man as the one getting married. Who are they to think their selfish interests take precedence over worship of G-d? But why am I talking to a boy!"

My head was spinning and I longed to see Mariamne again. She would understand my turmoil and doubts.

CHAPTER 7

Love postponed

Yohanan kept me waiting all summer. I would have lost all hope except for the fact that he and Clophas had occasional conversations when they met as we walked home at day's end. Shabbat was often a time to deepen friendships. And, always under observant eyes, Mariamne and I found time to share our deepest thoughts and joy-filled hopes.

The day I told her that Clophas had asked her father to consider a marriage between us, she showed no surprise. She responded in a way that was so natural I had to assume that she expected nothing less.

She was the first to say, "I love you. I want to spend my life with you, to have a family with you, to serve G-d with you." Waiting for a moment when her father was distracted, we stole our first kiss. In less than a second I was consumed in an eternity of love. She was soft and moist and responsive. I had never kissed another girl and knew there would never be anyone but Mariamne.

We dreaded the coming autumn. It made good sense for Yohanan to be in Capernaum during the summer. Situated on major trade routes, here was where he had the best opportunity to sell his salted fish and make contacts for the coming year. His two or three short trips to Magdala were necessary to check on catches and preparation, but his personal supervision over the winter was critical.

Finally the day before leaving Capernaum for the year, he invited Clophas, Mother, and me to dinner. As was their habit they rented a house close to the boats and market each year. His housekeeper had prepared the evening meal, and Mother had made arrangements with the neighbor next door to take care of the younger children. Counting Yaaqov bar Yosef there were five siblings now. In all there would be seven.

I was so nervous I hardly ate a bite. Yohanan had guarded his words all summer, never giving clear indication of what his answer would be. Mother said from the beginning, "Don't get your hopes up." But her tender caresses and dancing eyes could not assuage my uncertainty.

When at last dinner was over, we sat back, Mariamne beside her father across from me between my parents. A heaviness seemed to settle over the room while shadows from the lamp skipped on the walls. Through the windows I could see the countless stars and couldn't help silently uttering "Please, please."

After going on forever, I heard him say, "I have given great thought to your proposal. The differences that divide us become insignificant when compared to what we share. You are good people. You love Adonai as we love Adonai. I can't help but see the happiness in my daughter's face when she talks with Yeshua. And he can't begin to hide his affection for her when they are together. I accept your offer but…" I thought my heart would jump out of my chest.

"but what?" I silently repeated.

"but I must ask that we wait two years before there is a wedding. You know I do not have a wife or any other children. I need my daughter to run my household and, besides, she is very helpful with my business. I don't want to be negative, but I must be sure that she is well taken care of when I can no longer do it."

Of everything he could have said, this was both bitter and sweet. On the one hand I had the promise of life with the only person I ever loved besides my family. On the other hand the beginning and fulfillment of that dream had to wait. For a young man of seventeen, two years is a lifetime, and my passion for her was growing everyday. As our eyes met I knew she shared my longing. We knew our parents' agreement must be honored.

Father Yaaqov labored seven years for the woman he loved only to be tricked by a mikvoth he had forgotten. So he labored seven more years before experiencing the unfathomable love of Rachel. Surely two years won't be that hard!

While they seemed to never end, the years provided wonders and mystery.

I grew into manhood, taller, stronger, and guided by Clophas' skillful hands, more competent in my building skills. Mother's reservoir of love and compassion overflowed. I took great joy in her strength and guidance. We all delighted in the birth of Yehudah. In anticipation of the day when Mariamne would join our family, Clophas and I steadily worked on an additional room for the house.

Words cannot describe the transformation Mariamne went through. I had always thought of her as beautiful, but she blossomed into the most gorgeous young woman in Capernaum. I wasn't the only one to notice. Even when she teased me about all the attention the young men of Magdala or Capernaum showered on her, she always ended by squeezing my hand and, when possible, sharing a long, deep, promising kiss.

For a time, peaceful and unthreatened, we ignored the Romans or pretended they weren't there. As long as taxes were paid and no one violently challenged their presence, they left us relatively alone. I sensed an uneasiness but wasn't ready to acknowledge it. Every seventh year when debts should have been forgiven, the Romans scoffed at our Law and dismissed our protests. I wasn't sure how long G-d would wait.

As far as I was concerned He would have to. I was getting married.

CHAPTER 8

Foreshadowing

In the second summer of our engagement, Mother received word that her kinswoman Elizabeth who lived in Ein Kerem was ill. She had been a widow for seven years and lived with her son, my cousin Yohanan. He was born within the year before my birth, but we had never spent much time together. The five day journey from Galilee is not something you do that often.

Clophas thought it important that Mother visit her once more, and if I accompanied her, it would be an opportunity for me to worship in the Temple in preparation for my wedding.

When we arrived in Ein Kerem Elizabeth seemed to have improved somewhat. So, to take advantage of the time when we weren't needed, Yohanan and I made the short trip to Jerusalem. It gave us time to get to know one another better. In a word, he was intense!

"You know Adonai will not tolerate the desecration of Israel and the corruption of the Temple at the hands of the Sadducees. This evil age is coming to an end."

"What are you talking about? I know times are hard, but what can we do about it?"

"We must call G-d's chosen to prepare for the time when G-d will send his angels, annihilate the Romans, and restore the purity of the Temple."

"Yohanan, I've seen what war will do. I lost my father when he followed Yehudah the Galilean. Violence is not the way."

"I'm not talking about our violence; I'm talking about G-d's righteous violence. You know who we are and what our destiny is."

I was getting a little nervous with such talk. Oh, I want freedom and G-d's reign as much as anyone, but it had never quite gotten beyond wishful thinking.

"Mother has told me all about who you and I are. You come from kings and I am the descendent of priests. In the sacred texts it says a priest and a king will lead them and Israel will be restored."

"You've been spending way too much time alone in the wilderness. We're just boys and besides (pointing toward Jerusalem) what can we do against that, not to mention the Romans."

"You need to spend more time in the wilderness listening. Adonai has a purpose for you and me and we need to get ready. In 14 years it will be Jubilee. The prophet Daniel has told us when to be ready. The work is G-d's; we are His hands and feet. You and I, king and priest."

"My mother has told me the same stories. I'm just as proud of my ancestors as you are, but look at us. You've let the stories go to your head. Besides, I'm getting married when we return home. I don't have time to be a king."

We let the conversation drop for the time being. Zion stretched out in front of us, the most magnificent sight in the whole world. If only her heart matched her beauty. We stood, silent with our mouths open.

Because his father, Zechariah of the division of Abijah, served as priest before G-d, Yohanan had been to Jerusalem numerous times and was very familiar with his way around. Herod's palace, the praetorian, the gymnasium and public baths, the Kidron valley and Mount of Olives. Ascending the stairs to enter the Court of Gentiles, he pointed out Annas' house and, right next to it, what had to be Caiaphas' and Sarai's house. They were impressive, way beyond their seaside villa. Despite its architectural beauty (I would like to have had the skill to build something so grand) I had no desire to go inside, now or ever.

Once bathed, we passed through the Court of the Gentiles, the Court of Women, and entered the Court of Israel. I had anticipated the ritual requirements and with modest means purchased two doves for the burnt offering. After telling the priest of my plan to be married, he gave me the blessing and Yohanan and I quickly retreated. We had promised our mothers we would return before sun down and we were already late in leaving. In my ears the words of the prophet Micah were ringing—"What does Adonai require of you but to do justice, and to love kindness, and to walk humbly with your G-d?"

It was night fall before we arrived. Fortunately a full moon, the sun's handmaiden, illuminated the landscape. How glorious is the Father's creation, day or night.

Elizabeth had taken a turn for the worse about noon. Mother said she slipped in and out of consciousness all afternoon. Yohanan went to her side, wiped her face with a wet cloth, and tried to give her cool drink. Opening her eyes she smiled and, to my surprise, asked for me by name. It was a tender request and despite my reservations I quickly sat beside her opposite Yohanan. Lifting her hand she took mine softly.

"There is peace in your eyes and in your touch. I'm not afraid."

Those were her last words. Closing her eyes she seemed to relax. We sat without speaking for another watch, Mother joining us at her feet. And then without notice, she quietly died taking her place in the loving arms of Adonai.

The women prepared the body for burial, washing it, covering her with spices, and wrapping her in a fresh linen shroud. Yohanan and I took this time to walk together and share without speaking our deepest bonds.

Later Elizabeth was buried in what I learned was their family tomb. People in and around Jerusalem had started a new burial practice unknown to us in Galilee. After cutting a sufficient tomb in the soft rock, they also cut a loculus along one wall. The deceased was placed on the ledge and allowed to decompose over the next year and a half or two. Once the flesh was completely eliminated, the bones were collected and placed in an ossuary about the size of 1 cubit by 1 cubit by 2 cubits, sometimes larger if the bones of two individuals were buried together, sometimes smaller if intended for a child. Then the ossuary was placed in a niche chiseled into the side of the main room, if you could call it that. The last task was to seal the tomb in such a way as to protect it until needed again. Elizabeth was ultimately put to rest beside Zechariah.

It never crossed our minds that Yohanan would join them in 14 short years.

* * *

CHAPTER 9

Breaking custom

Someone said there are no accidents. Maybe not, but I prefer to think there are always opportunities. Adonai in His wisdom created us free to choose, to take the moment, good or bad, and make something better out of it. I knew people for whom things were so bad they gave up hope, whether it was their health, their relationships, or their faith in Adonai. Without hope there is no future. Without hope we fail to accept our responsibility and surrender to despair and darkness. Without freedom there is no love. Without love there is no meaning. Without meaning there is nothing.

And I love Mariamne!

We left Ein Kerem as soon as it was respectable to do so. Yohanan and I were only able to have short and practical discussions, but we both knew there was more that needed to be said. Mother politely invited him to move to Capernaum with us, but he insisted, ominously, there was much there he needed to do and assured us he would be fine. His parting word to me was, "Listen."

I suggested we head west toward Joppa and take the coastal road to Galilee. It would take an extra day but I thought it would be easier for Mother. She must have sensed my eagerness because she insisted that we head straight north through the heart of Samaria. I didn't fully understand the low esteem many fellow Jews held for the Samaritans. I was familiar with the history but all creatures stand equal in Adonai's eyes and love.

The hill country presented a challenge, yet Mother never complained. To be safe and avoid the occasional bandits roaming the countryside, we traveled with two other families in a group of twelve. The morning of the third day we skirted north of Mount Gerizim and soon came to the fork in the main road. One family bid us farewell and veered west to Caesarea. The remainder of the party turned north straight for lower Galilee. It wouldn't be the last time I traveled this road.

Our route took us to Nazareth, four miles south of Sepphoris. Memories flooded our hearts as we crested the hill and saw Nazareth before us. She didn't speak, but her tears told me how much she cherished the time she had spent here. Before long she was recognized and we were welcomed into the home of an old neighbor. I was ten when we left Nazareth at the beginning of the conflict.

"My how you've grown." "I don't recognize you." "You don't look a thing like your father, but I see your mother in your eyes and mouth."

I didn't care much for all the attention, but I was glad for Mother to have this time to share with friends and get a good night's sleep. The lines in her face and drooping shoulders told me she had just about reached her limit.

The road to the Sea was safe but we still needed one more night on the road before arriving home. With Mariamne in Capernaum and us not married yet, it was unthinkable that we impose on their household in Magdala.

When we did reach home midday, Clophas was off working and the neighbor was caring for the younger children. Yaaqov bar Yosef was old enough to work with us now, and he had gone with Clophas that morning. To no one's surprise the children were ecstatic to see their mother. I got a few hugs and kisses myself. When I look back, I know I was blessed to have a large, affectionate family. I guess that explains the joy and pain I would know later.

By summer's end the extra room was completed. Apologizing for not asking on the night of our betrothal, Yohanan came visiting one evening, as we found out later, to offer evidence of Mariamne's family purity and to ask about my own. Without hesitation Mother recited my heritage through Grandfather Heli through the priest Nathan, son of David, to Abba Abraham. She then told him, somewhat to his surprise, that my father had died when I was 10 going on 11 and that she had married his brother. Clophas had adopted me and Yaaqov. She also assured him that I was descended from David through his son Solomon and my father Yosef. She just didn't mention Tamar, Rahab, Ruth, and Bathsheba, trusting that if he knew the scriptures, he knew about David, Bathsheba, and Solomon. And if he didn't, well…

She smiled at me and I kept my mouth shut. If there were skeletons in Mariamne's family history, I didn't care or want to know. What matters is the present. Yohanan seemed satisfied.

With that burden lifted he announced that, unless we had objections, the wedding would be the first of Tishrei.

Having planned for almost two years, now there was a heightened sense of urgency. The wedding would be at our house. I could never repay Clophas' and Mother's generosity. Despite all the mouths they had to feed daily, he purchased a cow for the seven day feast and Mother prepared the house for the few guests expected to come and celebrate with us. Only the coming years revealed the boundless liberality of Mariamne's dowry.

She confided in me later, in playful private moments, of her wedding preparation. Yohanan's sister and their housekeeper woke her early, bathed her from head to toe, combed her long, flowing black hair, perfumed her exotically (that I discovered soon enough!), and dressed her in a new gown made especially for that day.

The procession from Magdala north to our house was accompanied by songs and music. Along the way people poured oil and wine in front of her to wish her health and happiness. There was even an occasional ear or two of roasted corn.

When they arrived at our residence, there was no chuppah. That was just a little more than we could afford. So, with most of the guests already present, they entered the house. As was the custom an opening blessing was given and, at the appointed time, the men gathered around the table Mother had so sumptuously prepared to take their reclining positions. They didn't notice that I had not taken my place until I interrupted their conversation.

"I know it is the custom only for men to eat at table on such occasions. But I want to break custom. Mariamne, Mother, come take your rightful places here."

There was stunned silence. You could have heard a shuttle drop. Clophas looked at me and then shyly smiled and nodded. Yohanan didn't know what to think, but he didn't object. Mother and Mariamne stood frozen like statues. Then when I stretched out my hand, they confidently came forward. Room was made for them. It didn't take long before everyone was engrossed in the most delicious food I had ever eaten. It wasn't my imagination because at every meal food and the best wine miraculously appeared with excess to share with neighbors. That was one of the happiest days of my life.

With blessings and subtle jokes only to be understood later, we were escorted to the room that had been prepared for Mariamne and me. The door was closed and after a few playful knocks, a song, and well wishes, the guests retreated to the far end of the house. Because the weather was so pleasant that time of the year, several chose to sleep under the canopy on the roof. For the first time in our lives, we were alone–together.

The muted glow of the single lamp provided more than ample light while the full moon showered our bed streaming through the high window. As would be the case about so much of our lives together, words were unnecessary. She snuffed out the wick and moved to the side of the bed waiting for me to join her. Her eyes beckoned me and her hands encouraged me eagerly. Without breaking our gaze I ran my hand through her long, loose hair and untied the belt from around her waist.

I remembered from days by the shore with the sun behind her and the wind gently blowing her robe to conform to her body that she was slender and full-breasted. I lifted the robe slowly over her head revealing her firm breasts and dark nipples. I had concentrated so intently on her that I didn't notice when she opened my robe and undid the sash holding my waist cloth. With tender and deliberate motion she pushed the robe off my shoulders.

I had had erections before. Haven't we all? But I had never felt such intense passion. When she took my penis in her hand and pulled me against her, our bodies melted into the oneness of the universe. Her skin was smooth and faintly scented from the morning's oil. Her perfume filled my head in perfect intoxication. In unison we silently fell to the bed like first snow. Previous kisses had been all too brief. Now we drank deeply. I caressed her body, stroking her thighs, kissing her navel, and molding her breasts. Between my fingers I felt her nipples harden and turn up to me, begging to be kissed. Her soft moans let me know that she shared my hunger.

Opening her legs, she gently urged me to take my place. Moon beams swaddled us in a welcoming embrace. The mysteries of the night were only beginning. I had never seen the hair between a woman's legs and had only assumed that they, like we men, had hair there. Mariamne's was dark, full, and inviting. Smiling, and whispering "Now," she took me in her hand and guided me into the most delicious pleasure I would ever know. Because it was her first time, she groaned and took me slowly in stages. And when I stopped and asked why tears, she kissed me firmly and told me pain always precedes pleasure, like a mother giving birth. Once the threshold is entered, the pain is forgotten. Joy and life enable us to endure anything, even death.

It wasn't long before I could tell the pain had gone. Deliberately, with enthusiasm she began to respond to my vigorous thrusts. And when I exploded her tongue filled my mouth to quieten my ecstasy. In that moment I touched the face of Adonai and shared the oneness for which we are created.

That was not the last time we made love that night, and each time was more pleasure-filled than the time before—without the pain. From that night forward we were never apart until the end.

A gentle knock on the door and Mother called us to breakfast. Smiling sheepishly at each other we dressed and tried to present ourselves to the guests as if nothing had happened. But when the shushin returned from inspecting our bed clothes and guaranteed the evidence of virginal blood, Mariamne and I both blushed.

CHAPTER 10

Innocence lost

As we settled into peaceful domesticity, I continued to work with Clophas and brother Yaaqov and Mariamne took her place beside Mother providing much needed help with children and house. Things were not so peaceful in Judea.

The year following our wedding, for reasons I never heard, Annas was removed from the office of High Priest by the Roman Prefect Valerius Gratus. He was replaced in short order by Ishmael bar Phabi, Eleazar bar Annas, and Shimon bar Camithus. Annas was a master of deceit and intrigue. Consequently he was never far from the seat of power. Few people were surprised when, three years later, his political maneuvering resulted in that same Valerius Gratus appointing Caiaphas, his son-in-law as High Priest. Caiaphas was the last High Priest I knew in my lifetime.

During the interim between Annas' and Caiaphas' rule, Caiaphas visited Capernaum one last time. By now he was a distinguished figure of Jerusalem society without time for a Galilean tekton. We spoke once. His tone was condescending, and when he realized that Mariamne and I were married, I didn't like the way he looked at her. His stare had an air of ownership and entitlement. She shuttered under his glare. Without a "shalom" he turned on his heel and walked away. Twelve years later we both remembered.

The summer of Caiaphas' appointment rumors floated throughout Galilee that Herod Antipas planned to build a new city in honor of Tiberius. It was to be south of Magdala on the coast. Always looking for steady work and a wage adequate for a young couple, I asked Clophas and Yohanan to find out what they could and let me know. Yohanan was able to confirm that, indeed, a city was being planned and, more importantly, Herod Antipas planned to move his administrative capitol there. Land preparation had begun and employment was available. This was a stroke of luck soon to be appreciated.

By now Yaaqov was a skilled laborer and carried his weight. Yaaqov bar Alphaeus was a youth but provided helpful assistance with menial tasks. Clophas would miss me but still encouraged me to look into opportunities there. Yohanan graciously offered Mariamne and me room in his house in Magdala enabling me to walk the short distance to work in the future Tiberias.

With the few possessions we had accumulated—bedding, a lamp, and tools—we moved in with her father. As I said, it turned out to be an opportunity in disguise. Shortly after moving Yohanan became ill. He lingered for a few months, but eventually died. Mariamne provided care and comfort; their bond grew stronger. And when he died, it was our love that kept her going. It wasn't the last time our love for each other and for Adonai brought vision and strength to our lives.

In the days and weeks that followed our love deepened and our love making gentle with purpose, and frequent. Work, sorrow, business details, household duties, maybe we were distracted. Maybe we didn't pay attention. Maybe we didn't know how to read the signs. After a week of not being hungry and throwing up every morning, Mariamne with girlish glee told me we were going to be parents. I knew it was possible, but I hadn't thought of myself as a father. And that night, lying in bed, I caressed her belly and saw the unmistakable rounded mound. Her size and beauty only grew.

Then that day, the day we would never forget, the day that changed our world, the day we lost our innocence.

We rose like any other day. By now the morning sickness had ended. As I left for Tiberias she mentioned that she had not felt the child quicken in her womb for three days but didn't want to alarm me. I asked if she needed me to stay with her but she assured me everything was alright. The child was probably resting; it had been very active for sometime. When I returned in the evening, I sensed an unnatural silence in the house.

Salome met me before I could enter.

"She's sleeping. It's in Adonai's hands."

She woke shortly, smiled lovingly at me with tears filling her eyes. The pains started again. Salome and the midwife placed her in the "travail chair" and comforted her all they could.

"What can I do?" I begged.

"Bring more heated water, some clothes, oil, and be sure the lamp does not burn out."

Waiting outside, her cries pierced my heart and I prayed. Reciting the psalms my thoughts returned to Mariamne and the unborn child. "Abba, please. Give me the pain. Spare her. She is your gift to me. With you she is my world."

For what seemed like an eternity, her cries continued. Until, with all sense of time forgotten, I realized her cries had ceased. I didn't wait and rushed toward the room. Again Salome met me at the door. Her face spoke a thousand words. In silence she fell at my feet and put her arms around me. I lifted her quietly and kissed her forehead, then entered the room. The midwife had finished cleaning Mariamne and had laid a small, motionless bundle beside her. Even after all that she had endured, there was a restfulness and acceptance on her face. I laid down beside her, rocking her slowly and waiting for her sleep to begin the healing.

It would have been a man-child, but it never drew a breath. Mariamne didn't want to disturb Mother; she had her hands full. But when Salome went early to tell her, they both returned before midday. The midwife was very capable. However, since Mother had had nine children all together, she knew what to expect and what to do. She assured us and herself that everything necessary had been done.

That day was spent in mourning. Mariamne and I simply sat, holding hands, occasionally a comforting kiss. The women prepared the evening meal and just as we gathered to eat, Clophas arrived. We hugged, and it was more affection than he had shown our wedding day.

"Trust in G-d," he whispered.

As was custom, as soon as Mariamne was able to move, our bed was lowered to ground level. The meal began with two cups of wine. During the meal we drank five cups, and after dinner we ended with three last cups.

A blessing was sung and for the first time I heard—"in the transformation, when Adonai calls us, we will all be resurrected to new life."

Early the next morning, with Mariamne's consent, I took the stillborn child, afterbirth and all, went to Nazareth and buried it with Abba Yosef. It was late when I returned, but she was waiting.

CHAPTER 11

Listen

Words are unnecessary. Too often, like smoke, they cloud our vision and confuse our understanding. If one is filled with G-d's word, only those with ears to hear will enter that realm. Only those open to G-d's breath truly live. Yohanan's last word to me—"Listen."

Mariamne and I didn't waste time with empty words. Our eyes and hands and bodies conveyed the deepest desires of our souls. We were confident there would be others, and if not, we would continue to live in the will of Adonai. So, without a word, life went on: working, fishing, loving, and "listening."

The daily walk to Tiberias provided plenty of time for reflection. While my hands helped build a kingdom on earth for Herod Antipas, my soul focused on the reign of G-d. Everyday testified to the cruelty of Rome and Herod Antipas' disregard for the welfare of his subjects. Taxes were a burden, always had been, but this project's cost was taxes and lives. With each increase more people starved and died. Homes and family land were surrendered to pay debts that mysteriously never disappeared. Children were sold into slavery, never to see their parents again. Had we been farmers I have no doubt that my family would have suffered the same fate. It was a meager existence, but there was always a need for common labor.

We decided early that the social distinction between servant and master was contrary to the will of Adonai. The chasm between wealthy and poor was inhuman, love-less, and unholy. After Yohanan's death Mariamne and I agreed to end the last vestiges of this in our house. Salome, her maid from infancy, was invited into the house with equal privileges. We knew the neighbors gossiped but noticed a change in practice on the part of a few. When one neighbor was evicted by a wealthy land owner, we took them in, man, woman, and child. When another villager was beaten to death by a drunk Roman soldier and his wife taken for the pleasure of the barracks, we took the abandoned child as our own. Before long a small community gathered, sharing earthly possessions and consciously, intentionally seeking Adonai's will in this world.

Mariamne learned well at her father's feet and after his death she continued to operate the business on a smaller scale. Some men refused to work for her, but others, especially those joining our "family" pitched in without a second thought. We didn't get rich; that wasn't our goal. But with the money earned and whatever others contributed to the common purse, we ate and clothed each other with no worry for tomorrow.

More and more frequently my walks home took me into the hills and isolated wadis. I often arrived home long after the others had eaten, but Mariamne did not chide or question. She "knew" and waited to share the meal with me. I didn't have to explain the pain I felt for the sufferings of G-d's people and the failure to follow His will. She heard the cries deep in her heart as well.

I wrestled mightily with the desire to escape it all, shut my eyes and ears to the prayers of the land for deliverance, to just enfold my family in the safety of our home, to provide for them, and avoid confrontation. Other times Mother's reminder of kingly roots and earthly power loomed before me. David had freed the people from foreign oppression, redistributed the land, brought the Ark to Zion in praise of Adonai. Why not me? Or better yet maybe I could lead the true Israel to Jerusalem. People are easily led. I could drive the profaners from the Temple, open the gates, and lead the nation in purified worship and genuine sacrifice. Everyone says I'm a natural leader.

Harah! How my head spins. And always, always—the words of the prophet Isaiah: "the L-d has anointed me—good tidings—afflicted—brokenhearted—liberty—open the prison—proclaim the year of the L-d's favor." Anointed me for what? I don't know! Frankly, where do the voices come from?

As if that weren't enough—"I know we put our lives in Adonai's hands and tried not to think 'maybe,' 'if,' 'possibly.' Yeshua, I'm pregnant." Holding her in a quiet embrace, a peacefulness settled over us and we knew, no matter what, this was G-d's will.

I would not be truthful if I said we didn't worry. All parents worry. "Will it be a boy or a girl? Will it be healthy?" Our question was, "Will it live?" With every glance and every kiss, the question went unspoken but filled the house more than sunshine. The only thing more consuming was our love for each other.

The day arrived and everyone was anxious. If she remembered the physical pain Mariamne did not voice it. The emotional pain was never far away. All anxiety vanished the moment I heard the first wail of exaltation. Greeting the world with such gusto that child almost woke the ancestors. I didn't wait to be invited and danced into the room. Tears of joy and relief, kisses of congratulations, prayers of gratitude. We had fulfilled the law of Moses—a son!

We were not superstitious, but we never speculated on its gender or discussed a possible name. When the midwife finished her tasks and the helpers left us alone, Mariamne, exhausted but exuberant, softly inquired, "What shall we name him?"

There was no hesitation. "His name is Yehuda. In him rests the hopes of the nation Judea." Her smile conveyed her consent. The child slept in her arms and she drifted to sleep dreaming of the day when Adonai's reign would be as real on earth as in heaven.

Following the commandment to "redeem before the L–d in the Temple," Mother and Abba Yosef took me to Jerusalem as soon as possible, offering two doves and receiving the blessing of the priest. We made the trip with Yehuda two years after his birth. By that time work had become scarce in the monumental capitol and the voice was compelling.

CHAPTER 12

Jubilee

I never cared for money. To me it was a means to an end, and that end was to share and provide for as many of G-d's people as possible. Once when the lawyers tried to entrap me, they showed me a coin and asked to whom it belonged. Those simpletons didn't begin to understand my answer. I told them to give to Caesar what was his and to give to Adonai what was His. In their blindness they thought I cleverly divided the earthly from the heavenly when, in fact, I challenged them to acknowledge that everything belongs to G-d; therefore, we owe everything to G-d. This is the whole basis of debt forgiveness and land distribution. When we live in the domain of Abba, there is a completely different economic system. This is Jubilee, the acceptable year of the L–d, transformation.

Even when I received wages for my labor in Tiberias, I gave the money to Mariamne and trusted her to share with those less fortunate around us. When we decided to travel south she took responsibility for putting the business in trusted hands and being sure that our "extended family" would be taken care of. She took a purse sufficient to provide for our small group of travelers, and we began our journey.

Like with Mother years before, I chose the road through Nazareth and Samaria to Jerusalem. For some time I had been yearning to see my cousin Yohanan again. I needed to tell him about the voice, to tell him I had been "listening," to learn about what he had been doing. When we arrived at Ein Kerem, a different family occupied the house I had visited. They said that some years before Yohanan had taken the Nazarite vow and moved to Suba. With guarded words, not knowing fully who we were or why we wanted to find him, they cautiously confided that he was said to be in the area of the Salt Sea. Some claimed he was possessed, others countered that he was a prophet. I was disappointed that he wasn't there anymore.

Sharing their hospitality, we rested a night and headed for Jerusalem the next morning. The work of a tekton is not conducive to wearing a tzitzit, but I was raised to honor Adonai, to pray three times daily, and to cover my head in perpetual reverence. I wore the tzitzit, prayed, washed my face and hands, observed the Shabbat—when the needs of G-d's creatures did not take priority. The spirit of the law made it clear that the Shabbat was made for man, not vice versa. I was appalled at the disregard for humility and brazen arrogance in Jerusalem. I told the others not to confuse human shortcomings with the legitimate admonitions of scripture.

The crowds are especially large during Pesah, so we quickly purchased our sacrificial doves, presented Yehuda to the priests, and headed for the Kiddron Valley away from the clamor and distractions. As we descended the stairs of the Temple entrance, a priestly procession was making its way up for evening prayers. I thought I recognized the priest at the head of the column. Our eyes met briefly in silent acknowledgement, and we each moved on just as we had moved on in our respective lives. The Kiddron provided safety, shelter, and seclusion. It wasn't a place the Romans concerned themselves with, and I returned more than once in the years ahead.

The following day I left the others resting while I wandered back into the city. With my head covered I could be as anonymous as I wanted, and I knew if I kept my mouth shut and ears open, I could pick up a lot of useful information. And I did!

Many of the people were talking about a prophet named Yohanan. Some said he was Elijah returned. Rumors were rampant but the consensus was that he had moved north. Many had sought him out, Pharisees and Sadducees. He railed against corruption and demanded that the people repent, all the people. It had to be my cousin, and I had to find him.

Returning to the camp, I told everyone what I had heard. Because it was already nearing sunset, we waited until the next day to start our journey. This time we followed the river road and the farther we walked, the more we heard about Yohanan the Baptizer. Over and over the multitude reported his simple message: "Prepare the way. Repent. The kingdom is at hand." I was dumbstruck by his directness.

If it hadn't been for the others, I would have kept going. But reaching Aenon just before dusk and seeing how tired Mariamne was, not to mention Yehuda, I decided to camp despite knowing that he was practically within a stone's throw away. The next morning we headed for Salem. When I inquired as to his whereabouts, they said he was down by the Jordan. My patience for rewarded, and I heard him before I saw him.

I don't know where they came from, but a huge crowd was gathered around him. We stood back listening and watching. One after another responded to his challenge. "Repent. Come and be baptized. Die to your old life. Live a new life. Enter the kingdom." This was different; this message was new. This wasn't daily purification; this was a new way to live.

Without being conscious of what had happened, I found myself at the edge of the crowd standing on the bank. Our eyes met in instant recognition. Before I could stop him, he pointed his finger at me and shouted, "There's the one from the house of David. I told you he was coming." And to me he said, "Shalom."

I stepped into the river and knelt in front of him.

"Are you sure you're ready?"

"I've been listening and I am absolutely sure."

He took my arms and pushed me under the liberating waters. And when I surfaced, it was as though a lifetime of uncertainty and selfishness was washed away. I heard the voice, the voice that hounded and haunted me for so long, whisper, "It's about time. You have work to do. Now listen to him." Yohanan had been on this journey a long time. He had much to teach me.

That night he shared our camp. While Mariamne and the others prepared the flat bread, he showed me where to find honey. He was very adept at living off the land. We talked long into the night after the fire died and others were asleep. We felt safe. After all, this was before Herod Antipas mounted his sister-in-law and Yohanan accused him to his face.

I told him what the people were saying about him, calling him one of the prophets. He had a good belly laugh over that one. I told him others were calling his followers "people of the Way," and with that he turned more serious.

"I only repeat what the prophet Isaiah said and tell the people to 'prepare the way,' I tell them to share their coats. How many can you wear at one time? I tell them to share their food. How much can you store before it spoils? I teach them to pray. All of this is to get ready."

"But how do you know? How can you be so certain?"

"Yeshua, I told you a long time ago. Listen! Open your eyes! The prophets told us. The Jubilee is upon us. Debts must be forgiven. Land must return to its rightful caretaker. Two moshiachs, two of Adonai's moshiachs will lead. We, you and me, must establish the kingdom. That's why you are here!"

I had never known anyone like him. Listening to him I was convinced and said, "You will save the world."

"Not me. Not you. Adonai. We are His vessels, His messengers. Don't let your ego get in the way," he occasionally reminded me.

"Yeshua, I've waited a long time for you. There is much work to be done. It's time to start."

Yohanan's closest disciples were Andrew, his brother Shimon, Philip, and Nathaniel. After some discussion he decided that since they had been with him longer, Andrew and Shimon would work with me. Besides, they were from Bethsaida. We would begin in the south outside Jerusalem, and Yohanan would stay in the north for awhile. We planned to meet here in early winter after Yom Kippur.

First there was a wedding to attend. Honestly I love a good party with food, wine, and friends. Any occasion to gather friends and share the earth's bounty is a good time. Combine that with a wedding and it's hard to beat. Yohanan didn't quite see it that way. He was seldom sociable, more serious and sober. His vow did not permit wine, and a sense of urgency weighed on his shoulders.

Nathaniel was getting married and we all were invited. He was from Cana. While not next door, it wasn't far from Capernaum and Mother could join us with some of my brothers and sisters. A couple of young men returned home to tell them about our plans and assist with the travel. The rest of us lingered for a day before heading for lower Galilee. Yohanan and I talked and dreamed.

It truly was a delightful wedding, and Nathaniel seemed genuinely pleased that we attended. I felt that life was about to take a significant turn and always the unknown followed me like a shadow. For now it was party time.

I was thrilled when Mother, Yaaqov bar Yosef, Yaaqov bar Alphaeus, Shimon, and Salome arrived. Everyone enjoyed themselves immensely. Other than the awkward moment when everyone thought the wine had run out and I lectured Nathaniel on kingdom etiquette, it was a wedding to remember.

"How long have you been with Yohanan? Haven't you learned anything? Nathaniel, the fruits of the earth are for all to enjoy. Don't hold back; share the best first. We haven't been promised tomorrow. If tomorrow doesn't come and I have shared all I have with others, I have no fears." For the moment Mother seemed slightly puzzled.

Yaaqov always looked up to me. I really don't remember having one cross word with him, but on the journey east the next day, he made the time to walk alone with me.

"Are you sure you know what you're doing? Frankly the reports about Yohanan are disturbing. He's drawing attention; it isn't all good, and now you're joining up with him? You've always seemed level-headed to me Yeshua, but I'm beginning to wonder. You have a wife, a child, a business you could run. Have you thought about all that?"

Salome closed in behind us and remained unnoticed until she spoke. "Even Mother has expressed concern."

"No one asked you, Salome. Go back with the women," Yaaqov snapped at her. I wasn't prepared for their challenge or attitude and finished the trip contemplating his words.

Rising early the next morning I did as I had so often and sought refuge in the hills outside Capernaum. In my dark moments the words of the psalmist soothed me and restored my strength. "I will lift up my eyes..." Time with Abba in prayer clarified my vision and I knew what I had to tell my family.

Before heading south to take up my work in Judea as Yohanan and I had planned, we gathered around the table for one more meal.

"You are my family. I have known you all my life, but I have felt for sometime that Adonai has a special purpose for me. You planted the seed, Mother. All your stories about Abraham and David ignited my imagination. You taught me that life's greatest purpose is to love Adonai and that the only way to do that is to love others, no matter how unlovely they can be at times." Smiling at her I continued, "You showed me in daily life that we love best by serving others. When we see His face in the faces of others, we can do nothing but love wastefully. Do not count the cost. Do not expect reward. Adonai loves us; let's love Him in deeds of kindness."

Yaaqov sat quietly offering no rebuttal. I wasn't sure he was convinced, but I knew I couldn't make him understand. Adonai created us with yetzer-ha-ra and yetzer-ha-tov. We have a choice. This is why I believe in free will. Without choice, there is no love. Love comes from the depth of our freedom. I know Adonai loves us and in freedom we love in return.

He gave me a strong and long embrace. Mother kissed us all and lingered with Yehuda. I almost sensed a sadness but decided not to prolong the separation. Yaaqov bar Alphaeus and Shimon begged to go with us; however, I knew they and Mother weren't ready...yet.

Shimon bar Yonah and Andrew got their house in order. Philip joined us from Bethsaida, and Yaaqov and Yohanan bar Zebedee, having earned the nickname of "sons of thunder" for their impetuous boldness, told their parents goodbye. It was a sabbatical year, and we would be in Judea in a week.

CHAPTER 13

Strategy at Wadi Cherith

As planned we rendezvoused with Yohanan east of Salim in the Wadi Cherith. When I reminded him that Elijah had fled here from the wrath of Jezebel, he had a generous laugh. "See why many think you are Elijah returned?"

"I'm not Elijah, but my message is the same. Israel must return to the worship of the G-d of Abraham and Yaaqov, or His wrath will rain down like the fire on Mount Carmel."

"Isn't that a little harsh," I asked with some hesitation.

With fire in his eyes he let me know in no uncertain terms, "There is an end to G-d's patience; He will endure only so much. Evil is loose in the land and good must prevail. Listen Yeshua, G-d spoke through Daniel. He laid it out unambiguously clear. At the end of 70 weeks, you know he meant years, it will be the appointed time. There are to be ten final Jubilees. Well, it is the final year. All things will be fulfilled.. Zechariah said, and Malachi confirmed, that a priestly moshiach and a kingly moshiach will lead the way. Damn it Yeshua, do I have to hit you beside the head with a rock! You and I have one message: the kingdom is at hand, it's imminent, and people had better get on board!"

If there had been any lingering doubts, they vanished. I felt his passion and I sensed it at the very core of my being. A house cannot survive divided. Either you serve Adonai or you serve mammon. There are no split loyalties, no part-time followers. You love Adonai with all your heart or you don't love Him at all.

We stayed a couple of weeks in that glorious place. It was safe and bountiful. The landscape was rugged but the caves provided shelter from rain, fires from the cold nights, fresh water from the numerous springs, edible vegetation, and meat from occasionally caught animals like rabbits and stray sheep. Even bandits avoided the wadi. Our community felt secure and at one.

Yehuda had a couple of playmates, and they were never beyond the watchful care of parents or other adults. An infrequent bee sting reminded them of potential dangers. There were so many caves that families had the privacy they wanted. Mariamne and I were not denied opportunities for the intimacy we treasured.

Yohanan and I filled long hours planning, sharing, and dreaming. His vision of the "end of the age" and G-d's re-creative transformation became clearer. We agreed that kingdom needed some organization; Yohanan and I would not be able to do everything. The role of disciples became crucial. Like Moses and the council of tribal leaders, we thought the restored kingdom would function best under twelve appointed leaders. Counting young Yosa, Shimon, Yaaqov, and Yehudah, who planned to join us the following spring, we had ten dependable candidates. Although they were young, Yohanan agreed to their inclusion because they shared my family history. Two more were needed.

For the remainder of that year Yohanan stayed in the vicinity of Aenon and Salim. He established quite a crowd of supporters. People from every walk of life went out to him, coming from miles away and traveling for days. Pharisees, Sadducees, Romans, inhabitants of Khirbit Qumran and the Decapolis. Understandably the authorities learned of him and, we were told, sent spies to keep a close watch. They weren't quite sure what to make of his message; it wasn't their history or religious perspective. For a time he seemed harmless enough.

I took a small band of followers and headed south into Judea. Maybe it was our accents that drew attention. Also a group of itinerant messengers was hard to ignore. Not that hospitality was unknown, but commensality and unselfish sharing, people who gave without demanding anything in return, were impossible to overlook. More importantly we encountered a hunger and thirst for Adonai's righteousness and good news of coming deliverance.

I remember the first man I baptized. I had watched Yohanan; he had baptized me. But watching and doing are two different things. Responding to my call to repent and enter the kingdom, this man bolted out of the crowd, fell at my feet, and demanded to be baptized then and there. We actually had to go looking for living water deep enough to enter. When we did, he was so excited and animated that he slipped out of my grasp and fell head long into the stream. I pulled him up sputtering while we all roared with laughter. I believe Adonai must have a good sense of humor.

Like Yohanan and his group we attracted a huge following from Jerusalem and the surrounding villages. My message set no limits or restrictions other than a sincere commitment to live under the reign of G-d. Rich or poor, man or woman, schooled or unlettered I challenged the house of Israel. And in the process a strange thing happened.

After a few weeks, and at the request of Nathaniel, I decided to take my message to Galilee. Traveling north through Samaria we arrived at Sychar. It was getting late so I asked Nathaniel and Philip to go into the town, along with Mariamne, and purchase some food for the evening. I stayed behind with everyone else so the children could rest and play. We waited by the well on the outskirts of town.

As we waited a woman came to draw her evening's water. My being a Jew and a man she did not glance at me or speak. It startled her when I asked her to give me a drink. She politely handed me a gourd full of water and said, demurely, "I'm surprised that you, a Jew, will speak to me, a married woman and a Samaritan."

"You certainly are a married woman, probably more than once." It didn't take a genius to assume that. She was in her thirties, had a painted face like women of the streets, and wore somewhat revealing clothes. Falling on her knees she exclaimed, "You must be the moshiach."

"It sure doesn't take much to impress you. I'm not the moshiach because I can tell you've been married more than once. That's easy. What I can tell you though is that there is living water to satisfy your thirst for meaning and purpose and you don't have to go to the well for it everyday. It is a gift from Adonai. His kingdom is coming and you had better get ready."

"Wait right here. Don't go away." Without her jar she ran headlong back to the village. Shortly I saw her returning along with several other neighbors. "That's him, the one who knew I had been married before."

Once they got over their desire for tricks and magic, we talked until sunset. Mariamne and the others had returned and jumped into the conversation. I didn't want to assume or impose, so I said we needed to be going before it got too dark. To their astonishment and some of ours, the woman from the well just blurted out, "Come stay with us. You look tired; the children need rest. We can make room for you." It was two days before we continued north to Galilee. The house of Israel should be so receptive!

The lower Galilee was fertile for the message of the coming kingdom. Its history with the Davidic family and the folklore, authentic and imagined, around messianic pretenders, created a sense of expectation so real you could reach out and grab it. Even among rural, simple villages news travels fast. They had heard about us and anticipated our arrival. People yearned to see and hear my message. It was heady stuff. I confess to enjoying the adulation. Thank goodness Mariamne was there to keep my feet on the ground.

Those early years in Capernaum were to prove very beneficial. Curious and awed by the power, knowledge, and "forbidden" attraction of the occupying Romans, I stole moments to walk among them and listen to their strange tales of far-off places and different cultures. They weren't threatened by a young Jewish peasant, so my access was virtually unlimited. The most fascinating aspect of their lives and practices was their medicine. On several occasions I observed the Roman "surgeon" straighten broken bones, open abscesses to excise horrible smelling fluids from abdomens, and even return sight to the blind by sucking objects from eyes through a glass tube. It was nothing short of miraculous.

While some of us were familiar with the torah of the Lawgiver relating to ritual purity and personal hygiene, we had never learned or implemented broader, community practices outside urban centers to keep down diseases and improve the quality of life for everyone. Mikvah for ritual purity are one thing; clean drinking water and isolated human and animal waste and garbage are quite another. I saw this in Capernaum and Sepphoris and wondered why this "knowledge" wasn't shared with all the people.

There had been a couple of times when people with afflictions, real and imagined, physical or mental, came to me and after being touched, left claiming to be healed. I tried to tell them that I could not heal their bodies but Adonai would make them whole in spirit, forgiving their sins. Some went away shouting but soon forgot the call to submission; others clung to the good news for a time but gradually settled back into old routines. A few came to fullness and wholeness.

Nathaniel, using Cana as his base, quietly and steadily built a community of disciples preparing them for the coming day of the L–d (Yom YHWH). It was convenient to visit and rest for a few days after the time in Samaria. It was while we were there that an official from Capernaum who heard we were back in Galilee came looking for me. He was the same official whose house Clophas and I had worked on. We had remained friends, as close as master and subject, Roman and Jew can be.

I detected he was anxious and at the end of his rope. He related how his son had become very ill after dinner three days earlier. As we talked and he shared what he remembered, what they ate, how it was prepared, what the boy had done before that afternoon, his fear subsided. Surmising bad food, bad preparation, or too many green apples before dinner, I recommended a couple of healing herbs and encouraged him to return home quickly. I learned later of the boy's recovery and confession. He learned the hard way about parental wisdom.

It was an amazing summer. A couple of short trips to Magdala relieved any concerns about the community or the fishing. Morale was high; generosity was boundless. I traversed the lower Galilee delivering the message of transformation, freedom, call to covenant faithfulness. Sure, there were those who selfishly sought forgiveness of debt and the return of the land to rightful owners. They didn't understand that the true owner of the land was YWHW and we are but custodians. They reveled in the belief that the goim would be expelled and all nations would be subject to a restored Davidic king. They longed for a cataclysmic, devastating annihilation of the foreigners. They only saw the externals, blind to Isaiah's servanthood and Jeremiah's covenant of the heart. When I refused to encourage an assault on Sepphoris or Tiberias, many withdrew in disillusionment. Uncertainty, hope, patience, or the absence of alternatives—the crowds grew and waited.

Naively I ignored the signs.

* * *

CHAPTER 14

Healing, helping, and hurting

The harvest was bountiful—crops and people. As the Feast of Dedication approached, Mariamne and I decided to go to Jerusalem, allowing time to stop by Yohanan's camp at Wadi Cherith.

Despite his intense focus and single-mindedness, it was invigorating to be with my kinsman. He related stories of compelling success, how throngs came to him in the wilderness, rich and poor, commoner and aristocracy. I told him about the eagerness and anticipation building in the Galilee. Yet beneath it all I sensed an agitated and impetuous spirit. Like others Yohanan was impatient. He trusted G-d; he put the pending conflict into G-d's hands. But he wanted it yesterday. I shared his vision; I shared his commitment to G-d. I knew the Day was coming. Unlike Yohanan, I trusted G-d's timetable, not ours.

Differences acknowledged, pledges renewed, Mariamne, Yehuda, and I with a handful of followers so as not to attract too much attention continued down the river road to the City of David.

Skirting the city to approach it from the south, we entered by way of the Huldah Gate. As was their custom many poor and sick gathered at the gates in hopes of a few shekels or who knew what else. It was Shabbat, and hoping to slip into the Temple without distraction, we blended in with other pilgrims hardly slowing down.

Unexplainably, unavoidably, our eyes met and he addressed me directly. Something about him would not let me escape. Kneeling beside him beside the pool Bethzatha, my heart swelled with compassion. He told me about a life of pain, rejection, and dis-ease. We spoke softly, passionately. I listened and in his voice I heard the voice of G-d. Accept-love-serve. To my amazement he slowly, gently got on his knees, gathered his pallet and cloak, and vanished into the crowd. The consequences presented themselves soon.

Those with me murmured among themselves; I ignored their questions. Mariamne's eyes held all the meaning and understanding I needed. Once inside the Temple and against her protests about why it was not time to challenge custom, Yehuda and I continued to the Court of Israel.

Imagine my consternation immediately upon entering when the man from the pool ran at me shouting, "That's him! That's the one who healed me." In spite of my insistence that G-d, not I, had healed him, I could tell the situation held potential danger. Amid shouts and accusations, I heard angry charges of "healed on Shabbat," and something about blasphemy and claiming equality with G-d. I had no desire to put Yehuda in jeopardy, so I quickly grabbed him and managed to get out without detection. Mariamne had heard the commotion and wondered what was happening. Fortunately I remembered where we parted and her insistence not to move. Grabbing her by the hand we eventually found our way to the south portico, out the Huldah Gates, down the stairs, and headed for the Kidron Valley where I knew we would be safe.

Yaaqov bar Yosef was the most pious and peaceable of all my brothers. He had volunteered to remain in Jerusalem, leading and nurturing the small community that was gathering there. He also wanted to be near the Temple, and while he shared our vision of a transformed world, he was even more patient than I in trusting G-d to bring the kingdom in His own time. He opened his home, shared with others, and provided the shelter and privacy necessary. It wasn't time yet.

After a month or so when the excitement of Dedication had died down, I gathered my family and handful of co-workers, left by way of the Mount of Olives, spent a night in Bethany with dear friends Mary, Martha, and Lazarus, and headed north to Magdala traveling on the east side of the Jordan.

Our home in Magdala and Shimon's home in Capernaum (he had relocated sometime ago from Bethsaida) provided havens for rest and centers for preparation for the coming days. While Mariamne supervised the business as only she could (Abba Yohanan had taught her well but she had tremendous natural ability), Philip, Shimon, Nathaniel, Yaaqov bar Alphaeus, and I covered the Galilee, preaching in every village, calling the people to prepare for the coming kingdom. Shimon's house gave Mariamne a home away from home when she needed to be in Capernaum for business. They were a second family.

And Yehuda! What can I say about that boy? He grew before my very eyes! I longed for him to inherit a world free of strife, a world in which all needs are met and all of G-d's creation exists in harmony and faithful observance of G-d's will. He would remain an only child, the embodiment of our history, our hope for the future.

Yohanan's, and to be truthful Shimon's, vision of quick and catastrophic commencement of the kingdom was tempting. Sometimes the pain and suffering of G-d's chosen was so overwhelming my patience wore thin. When the am-ha-aretz have lost their land, sold their children into slavery, paid rent, taxes, and Temple obligations, they have a difficult time waiting on G-d to restore justice, bring the haughty low, raise the oppressed. I shared their deepest yearnings, but my line was razor thin between despair and armed conflict. I had seen enough death and carnage in Yehudah the Galilean's failure. I had seen enough of the Roman's brutality. I had lost a father.

Because of the incident in the Temple last Dedication and the pressing demands at home, I chose not to go to Jerusalem for Pesah. Besides, Yohanan and I needed a little more time to plan the appropriate time to march on Zion.

One day, responding to the pleas of the Geneserets, we left Capernaum and went to the other side of the Sea. The multitude had gathered and was waiting for us. Finding an outcropping on the side of a sloping hill, I found a place to sit and shared my vision of needs met and faithful obedience to G-d's will as given through Moses. My view was of the law given for us, Shabbat for our rest and praise of G-d in service to others. I told them that the kingdom is even now breaking into our world if they would only open their eyes and accept the mandate to be G-d's hands and feet.

Just when I thought they might be getting the message, Philip reminded me, "Yeshua, it's midday and they're hungry."

"What has that got to do with me?"

"Well, they came to listen to you, and they expect you to take care of them," Philip replied.

Looking over the crowd I had to bite my tongue. "Are you so thoughtless that you came all the way out here without bringing food? Are you so concerned about yourselves and so selfish that you can't see the needs of those around you? You brought nothing into this world. All you have comes from above. You'll take nothing from this world. Why can't you open your hands and hearts and share without thought of return?"

Slowly, one by one, they opened their cloaks and shared their provisions, bread and fish, wine and olives. Then out of embarrassment or genuine feelings, they began to shout.

"Hosanna. King Yeshua. Son of David. You are king. Down with the Romans."

They were beyond reason. All hell broke loose. There was no calming them.

I managed to cloak myself and vanish into the mob. Needing time alone for reflection and solitude, I decided to walk back. It would take longer traveling the northern shore, skirting Bethsaida, and returning by the paved via but my head was spinning.

"King Yeshua.

Long live king Yeshua.

How easy to forget I'm only a man."

The disciples felt impotent as well, and without my guidance they weren't sure what to do. Making their way back to the boats, they sailed west. Dusk was falling as they drifted within sight of Bethsaida.

I have always loved the Sea and swimming was a favorite past time. The waters are clear, cool, and refreshing. The marshes of Bethsaida provide privacy. I abandoned caution, stripped to my loin cloth, and waded in. It must have been just what I needed because I became lost in awe and wonder. "Why do we worry so much about what to wear or what to eat? Abba provides food for fish and fowl. He adorns lake and land with breath-taking beauty. If we only trusted!"

I was so oblivious to distractions around me that I failed to see the approaching boat and the disciples waving frantically. By the time I did see them and had collected my clothes, they had beached the boat nearby.

"You gave us quite a scare," said Philip.

"I thought you were either a ghost or were walking on water," exclaimed Shimon.

"It sure doesn't take much to impress you idiots. Let's get home," I said smiling.

* * *

It was morning by the time we arrived in Capernaum. The crowd finally realized we had left them. Some taking their own boats came to Capernaum looking for us. With cooler heads prevailing, and because it was Shabbat, synagogue provided the perfect place and occasion to discuss my message and meaning.

The reading for the day was about Moses and the manna in the wilderness. Even when I tried to distinguish my message of the kingdom as eternal bread from the perishable kind, they did not fully grasp the significance. Even the leaders of the synagogue, supposedly wise and spiritual, missed the point and began accusing me of claiming equality with Moses and G-d! They openly attacked my social background, as if G-d cares, reminding those present that I was the son of Yosef from Nazareth. Nazareth of all places! They totally distorted the analogies of heavenly bread and earthly manna, physical flesh and spiritual oneness with G-d.

And they were convincing. Many quietly turned and walked away. Others were more vocal and even threatening. I was blind not to recognize potential danger and betrayal. But up here, far removed from Jerusalem, I felt safe. The reports from Judea were not as encouraging.

* * *

CHAPTER 15

Patience wears thin

It was an uneasy summer. I was unable to mask my internal tension. I must have been short tempered and short worded. Mariamne sensed it but waited patiently for me to open conversations. Even Yehuda seemed to know something wasn't right and left me with my thoughts.

There were reports from Judea. Food riots more frequent. Stone throwing in Jerusalem. Brutal crowd control by the Romans. Open conflict between Yohanan and the religious authorities despite his well-placed defenders.

As Sukkoth drew close my brothers became more insistent on marching to Jerusalem. Even young Yosa and Yehuda were caught up in the fever.

"It's time! It's time now!" they said.

Why they continued to wait and look to such an ambivalent leader is beyond me. Finally in desperation or just to buy time, hoping for a sign, I convinced them to go ahead. I asked them to consult with Yaaqov and read the mood of the crowds as objectively as possible. I promised I would join them at the Mount of Olives camp and made them vow not to do anything until I arrived.

After a week Mariamne, Yehuda, and I turned south. We avoided attention by traveling with a small group, and arriving in Jerusalem the day before the Feast began, we constructed our booth among the throng gathered to celebrate. I really did not intend to create a confrontation. All I wanted was to worship quietly, prayerfully. "My house shall be a house of prayer for all people."

The callousness of the Sadducees was more than I could stomach. Solomon's Porch was nothing but a market place. More than once I saw the Temple treasurers cheat the peasants as they exchanged goods and coins for proper shekels. What the am-ha-aretz broke their backs to produce for offering to G-d was taken by Romans and pilfered for the luxury of the Temple priests.

As I stepped out and spoke up a crowd began to gather around me. Soon I recognized familiar faces from the Galilee and from the communities in the Kidron and Mount of Olives. Fearing loss of control the authorities restrained the Temple Guard counseling restraint until backup could arrive. When the Guards did arrive, they were hesitant to follow orders or arrest anyone. They knew they were outnumbered. One thing in their favor was the disagreement among the crowd over my role and authority.

There was open talk of rebellion. Words like "moshiach" and "coming king" were thrown around, but in the absence of physical violence, the guards were reticent. They seemed to enjoy debating whether a moshiach would come from Galilee or Bethlehem. Whatever the reason, I was untouched and the authorities just got angrier and angrier.

Mariamne took my arm and we left. Down the stairs and out the Golden Gate, we headed for the Mount of Olives. With those who chose to follow, the Mount of Olives provided safety. She was concerned for my well being, but Yehuda had her full attention. He had been seen and identified with me. She sensed his future was in jeopardy.

To make matters worse and incite the multitude more, news arrived that Herod Antipas had arrested Yohanan and sequestered him in his palace at Macarias. The differences between Yohanan's aggressiveness and my counsel for patience only simmered while the two of us went about our work. When it seemed that my followers outnumbered his, he never showed jealousy or anger, but I still felt that he continued to harbor the desire to "force" G-d's hand in a final Armageddon.

Once Herod mounted his sister-in-law like a wild stallion, Yohanan could not keep his mouth shut. He accused Herod of adultery to his face—he was right!—and called Herodias a whore—right again!. Herod was not going to be publicly insulted without retaliation, and Herodias' pride demanded an answer. So there he sat in Herod's prison.

Everything that happened—Temple, Yohanan—gave me the opportunity to address our differences and try to channel the crowd's energy for the right time and place.

"Real freedom, true freedom comes from G-d. All of man's efforts are futile. Even David's greatness came to nothing when G-d's will was forgotten. Power, wealth, control vanish into thin air when they come from man's desires. The land is G-d's; we are only stewards. We are not here to fatten our bellies and fill our treasuries. G-d doesn't want burnt offerings and hollow praises. We worship G-d when we provide for the widow and orphan, heal the sick, feed the hungry, shelter the homeless, welcome the stranger. The kingdom of G-d is at the door. The call has been heard in Galilee, the Kidron, Aenon, and here. Open your eyes. Open your ears. Open your hearts."

Shimon leaped to his feet, drawing his sword from inside his robe. "Yes! Now!"

"Dammit Shimon. Haven't you heard a word I've said?"

Responding to Shimon's example some within the crowd challenged my words. "Are you a Samaritan? You act like a weakling. Are you possessed by demons that make you afraid? Why not now?! You mamzer. Where's your backbone?"

Two of them forced their way toward me with daggers drawn. I confess to being glad Shimon was beside me with that sword of his. A Pharisee was heard to mutter, "Too bad they didn't kill the mamzer so he could enjoy his resurrection and we could get on with the business of liberation."

I knew Yohanan's followers at Aenon and Salim were anxious, so I decided to make my way north. Things needed to settle down in Jerusalem.

CHAPTER 16

Dead or Alive?

Winter came early that year. It was brutal, and while the Wadi Cherith was well protected from Roman incursions, it could not keep out the cold. Mariamne was patient and did not complain once. However, when Yehuda became ill and his fever lasted for two days, I could tell she was anxious. With some effort despite her protests, I convinced her to take the boy to Magdala where Mother could help and she could get some much needed rest. A break in the weather enabled her, Yehuda, Yosa, Yehudah, and a half dozen others to make the short but grueling journey.

Mother yearned to see her youngest and to get a report on her oldest. For fear of her safety I insisted that she oversee the family in Magdala and be spared the potential danger in Jerusalem. There was no question about her commitment to our mission; after all she had named her sons to keep the memory alive. Approaching fifty after having nine children, her strength was not what it once was. Her desire for the kingdom had not diminished one bit!

Mother was well-placed in Magdala to nurture the disciples, oversee the finances of the business, guarantee provisions got to us as needed, and, from that safe distance, stay informed about Roman activity in the area. As Magdala was the source for much required salted fish, Mother was not once suspected of opposing their presence or desiring their removal. Nathaniel relied on her to keep him aware of our movements down south. His success recruiting in Tyre, Cana, and Kochba was crucial and proved to have long term consequences. He worked well with Philip, and the latter's success in Bethsaida, along with Bartholomew, gave energy and enthusiasm that kept us going. It was time to test the waters again. While I trusted G-d to bring the kingdom in the ripeness of His time, my mission was to prepare the way and call His people back to covenant faithfulness.

"The kingdom is at hand. The Day of the L-d draws near. Open your hearts!"

Three months had passed since Sukkoth. The Feast of Dedication was approaching. With Shimon, Yohanan, and Thaddeus I decided to return to Jerusalem. For better or for worse, after nearly three years of preparation my presence did not go unnoticed. Followers from Bethany and the Kidron rushed to the Temple when word reached them that we had arrived. Disciple and doubter alike demanded verification.

"Is it time? How long are you going to keep us guessing? Where is your army? When do we take back the Temple from those corrupt hands? Are you the moshiach, the one we have been promised?"

Pharisees and certain of the authorities insisted, "Are you the one to restore Israel?"

"You blind idiots! Look around you. Can't you see how desperate the people are for freedom? Can't you see and feel the suffering of G-d's people? Aren't you incensed at the injustice that stalks the land? Don't you hear the cries rising from spilled blood of the martyrs? G-d is not deaf! G-d is not blind!"

Shimon, ever vigilant, was the first to notice. "Rabbi, it's time to go. This is getting out of hand, and we are outnumbered." A few stones were thrown, drawing the attention of the Temple Guard.

Shielded by their bodies, bruises we nursed later, we forced our way through the mob, down Solomon's Portico, and out the Susa Gate. Stupidly we headed straight for Bethany and the home of Mary, Martha, and Lazarus. I later regretted exposing them and the followers in the village to the grave danger that was coming. Fortunately the wounds were superficial, and I realized we could not stay.

We no sooner arrived at the camp at Aenon and Salim than word reached us of an attack on Lazarus. Our friendship had not gone unnoticed, and a hand full of cowards cornered him, beating him within an inch of his life, leaving him for dead. When they found him, Mary immediately sent word. It still took two days before I was able, against the advice of everyone, to return to Bethany.

Martha and Mary were convinced that it was hopeless. They had even begun preparation for Lazarus' burial. It was subdued, but in their grief I knew they held me responsible for what had happened to him. Arriving at dusk I immediately went to where Lazarus lay in a coma. Despite Martha's and Mary's attention to his wounds, I almost didn't recognize him. He was swollen and discolored from the stoning and multiple blows he had received. When the others left us alone, all I could do was weep. "Am I responsible for this? Is it all worth this?"

Alone with my friend, holding his hand, caressing his face, I prayed—all night. As the sun rose I was awakened by the slightest squeezing of my hand. Raising my head I saw Lazarus staring intently at me with a smile on his lips. After putting water to those parched lips and giving thanks to Adonai, I called his sisters.

"Martha. Mary. Our brother has returned to us."

People have a way of believing and seeing things their own way. The rumor spread quickly that I had raised Lazarus from the dead. Others, less dramatically, were simply relieved that he had not died. The authorities saw the episode as superstition and a further incitement to the incendiary conditions that were building.

I was convinced of the necessity to retreat, at least temporarily, and to protect my followers in the vicinity. I quickly headed for Ephraim to regroup. Word reached us that the High Priest was reported to have said that it would be much better for one man to die than the nation suffer as a whole. It was public knowledge that he put a price on my head. When that notice reached Magdala, Mariamne left Yehuda in Mother's care and traveled south. Trusting G-d can lead to dangerous decisions.

CHAPTER 17

What does it take?

In Ephraim I felt like we would be safe long enough to make our final plans. The Council of Twelve were assembled; anticipation reached a fevered pitch. What happened next was unbelievable.

* * *

CHAPTER 18

Losing our heads

Exhausted and breathless, Eliazer collapsed at my feet.

"He's dead."

"What are you talking about?" I asked.

"Yohanan, he's dead."

Stunned, I stared at him. No one else uttered a word. With every eye in the room on me, I stood speechless, mouth open, trembling. Only when Mariamne slipped her hand in mine did the world begin to come into focus again.

"Sit," she said quietly.

Of course there was concern when Herod Antipas arrested Yohanan, but his indispensable role, the necessity of his partnership never let us think any harm could come to him. His father's Temple associates had petitioned for his release, advising against anything that would further incite his followers. I heard that however distasteful it was to him, Herod was contemplating releasing him.

"What changed his mind?" I asked in disbelief.

"Herodias demanded satisfaction," he replied.

It would take time for the meaning and implications of Yohanan's death to sink in.

A priestly moshiach to lead in covenant renewal.

A kingly moshiach to restore the nation and initiate G-d's law in kingdom law.

Together, Adonai's anointed.

Silence.

CHAPTER 19

Mariamne's faith

Was he wrong? Some claimed Yohanan was crazy. After all, too much time in the desert eating locust and flat bread can make a man do and say strange things.

Was I wrong? There's such a fine line between complete devotion and fanaticism. Before long a person can't tell the difference between G-d's will and their own personal obsession. Good ancestors do not a moshiach make. It can be very difficult to know who promises provisions, safety, and power. Adonai or Satan?

"Do I need this? Do I want this?"

"Yeshua, I've known you since I was a girl. I have never doubted your sincerity or your humility. I have embraced your message as you have. Now is not the time to stumble," Mariamne confided.

"Yeshua, you are the moshiach, the one anticipated since the fall of Jerusalem and promised by the prophets. Yohanan, Elijah, has spoken. Now is the time to act," counseled Shimon.

I cannot claim that all doubt left me. Neither can I claim that I never looked back or questioned the decision made. But in that moment I turned my face to Zion and the goal I believed Adonai had put in front of me.

It was decided. The excitement was palpable.

The Twelve would return to their respective districts and prepare the people for the march on Jerusalem. With Mariamne and Yehuda I would return to Bethany. Martha, Mary, and Lazarus insisted that we stay there. Jews and Romans would be overwhelmed by the sheer numbers of followers as they converged on the city. Coming from Galilee, Samaria, Judea, east of the Jordan, and the Negev, G-d's people like their ancestors led by Abba Yeshua would rise up and the walls of Roman hegemony and Jewish hypocrisy would crumble. The hosts of YHWH would take Jerusalem and the kingdom would know no end.

Six days before Pesah I took my family and slipped into Bethany under cover of darkness. Everything must be in place. Everyone must do their part. The stage was set.

"We have waited and suffered a long time. Who would have dreamed that we would witness this day! Above all generations we are most blessed." Lazarus' enthusiasm was boundless.

"Abba, your kingdom come on earth. Your servants wait," I prayed.

SECTION III:

Climax

CHAPTER 20

Pesah problems

Yeshua was a brilliant strategist. His humble demeanor was deceiving. While Yohanan never left anyone wondering where he stood or what he thought, Yeshua was a master at manipulation or persuasion, depending on your perspective.

Shabbat before Pesah put the plan in motion.

Intentionally embodying the words of the prophet Zechariah, Yeshua chose a young colt to ride as he entered Jerusalem. The Twelve had been instructed to infiltrate the crowd and, as Yeshua passed by, incite them with shouts of "Hosannah, son of David." Followers were to converge on Jerusalem during the five days before the Day of Preparation. Yeshua would spend those days in the Temple preparing the people and challenging the authorities. Then exactly at noon on the Day of Preparation, as the High Priest was to slaughter the paschal lamb, Yeshua and the Council would storm the Holy of Holies, throw the doors open, rip the curtain down, and pray for the coming of the L–d.

Jerusalem swells with worshippers especially at Pesah. It was not unusual for the streets to be packed and emotions high. As precaution the Prefect Pontius Pilate came from Caesarea Maritima; this time with an extra cohort of the 6th Legion for crowd control. This festival, with its emphasis on national identity, was always a concern. Pilate, true to his reputation of brutality and no nonsense, always erred on the side of excess in his effort to remind the Jews who was in the power seat. On such visits he stayed in the Great Palace of Herod from which he could personally monitor crowd movement and mood. He was well-informed about past messianic revolts and had no intentions of letting such a thing happen during his administration. But even the Roman Empire had limits to its harshness and standards of efficiency in the implementation of its laws. Pilate would cross that line one day, but not now.

Surprisingly, if the Romans were alarmed by the massive numbers gathered this year, they showed restraint. But restraint did not mean they weren't concerned or prepared. Extended conversations with the High Priest Caiaphas and Annas, his father-in-law and predecessor, had identified an itinerant "prophet" from Galilee as a potential trouble maker. His assumed relationship with Yohanan the Baptizer, recently beheaded by Herod Antipas, only intensified the situation. It was enough to bring Herod to Jerusalem in a demonstration of greater collaboration (and servitude). Rome, Temple, and Jewish Governor stood shoulder to shoulder.

Given planning, preparation, and anticipation, the swell of the multitude that Shabbat forced the authorities to soberly reflect on a more appropriate time and place to remove the cancer. Having positioned Roman soldiers on the walls surrounding the Temple throughout Solomon's Portico, Pilate, Herod, and Caiaphas stationed themselves in the Tower of the Trumpets and absorbed the spectacle below. From this vantage point it was quite easy to identify the center of activity.

Yeshua left Bethany early by the third watch. He chose a route down the Mount of Olives, gathering followers at every point along the way. By the time he rounded the southeast corner of the Temple Mount and reached Herod's Porch, the push of the throng threatened to crush him. With great effort the Council around him was able to hold back the ecstatic mob and enabled him to climb the stairs and enter the Court of the Gentiles through the Huldah Gate. He moved quickly talking first to this group and then to another.

Two episodes particularly caught the attention of the triumvirate. Although they couldn't hear the conversations, the animated responses of the listeners told them something significant was being discussed. Their spies informed them that evening that one group was emissaries from the

Decapolis. They had petitioned Yeshua for a role in power sharing when something called "the kingdom" was established. The spies were unable to confirm Yeshua's response, but the Greeks seemed to have retreated slightly confused.

The other incident had to do with paying taxes. This time the spies were emphatic regarding Yeshua's response. "Give G-d what belongs to G-d first. Then anything left over you can give to Caesar." They were sure he smiled and continued, "Obviously nothing will be left for Caesar!"

It was reported that he then moved through the Court of Women, even taking time to converse with several of them. His female companion, since this was as far as she was permitted to go, continued those conversations while he proceeded into the Court of Israel.

Caiaphas' ears perked up when the spies related how he verbally attacked the priests. He challenged their motives and sincerity, accused them of hoarding the offering brought to honor G-d, and even challenged the sacrificial system itself muttering something about mercy, justice, and humility. Fearing he might try to enter the Holy of Holies, a cadre of priests had clustered before the entrance just in case.

Incensed by what they saw and heard, the three pillars stormed their way through the Portico and down the stairs of the Antonia Fortress back to the Palace. Visibly shaken (or impressed) the collaborators realized the seriousness of the situation.

"I want two more cohorts in Jerusalem. Take these orders immediately to Caesarea. Be there by dawn! One is to come by way of the coastal road. At Joppa have them cut across lower Samaria to Jerusalem. The other is to cross the lower Galilee and come down the Jordan Valley Road. Double time if necessary but I want them here by three days time. Scare the "harah" out of these dumb peasants, and when they see the mighty Roman army coming from east and north, we'll see how brave these pilgrims are then," Pilate roared. As soon as the scribe completed the order and Pilate affixed the official seal sin cere, the messenger was on his way.

"In the meantime relocate half the praetorian guard to the Antonia. With the first show of violence, I want them through that passage and up those stairs into the Court of the Gentiles."

"My escort will camp south of my father's Porch in the Kidron to discourage any activity down there," Antipas offered.

"I'll put the Temple Guard on high alert and cancel all leaves of absence," Caiaphas added.

"I heard you tendered a reward for anyone who could deliver this pretender to you. What's come of that?" inquired Pilate.

"You know how those things are. Rumors are a denarius a dozen; opportunists come out of the woodwork. One fellow did interest us and we're waiting to see if he can do what he claims," Caiaphas answered. "What makes him interesting and us wary is that he claims to be part of this Yeshua's inner circle. He promised to keep us posted of his movements and, if the opportunity presents itself, share any information that might prove valuable. I told him he'd get paid when it happened! I'm not expecting much from him."

"Well, whatever. I'm telling you two right now that I will not tolerate the least threat or challenge to my authority. You can be prepared for a swift response," Pilate concluded as he dismissed the others. "It's imperative that we stay in touch. Be back here for an update tomorrow at sundown."

CHAPTER 21

Clouds gather

According to plan, the first day of the week Yeshua was back in the Temple. Despite being a festival week, this day found fewer worshippers on the Temple Mount. The usual merchants were there offering small animals and fowl for sacrifices and food for those hungry without their own provisions.

Less confrontational, more persuasive, ostensibly patient, Yeshua spent this day like the next four avoiding the soldiers and sharing his vision of a Jubilee, debts forgiven, land restored to "rightful" owners, sacrifices replaced by compassion and justice. It all sounded harmless as long as there weren't actions to back it up. More people dream than do anything.

Evenings were spent in Bethany or encamped on the Mount of Olives. The Twelve slowly drifted in with reports of their people arriving in Jerusalem, and Yeshua's confidence increased. To avoid drawing too much attention to themselves too soon in the week they chose to lodge in different homes or camps, no more than two together in a single place. However, it was decided that they would all meet at sunset, the beginning of Preparation, for the last strategy session. Yaaqov's house in the lower city near the Siloam Pool was designated as the place where the Council would eat one last time before gathering followers on the Mount of Olives for the morning's assault on the Temple.

Midweek reports of troop movements in Judea and throughout Galilee and the Jordan cast a sobering pall over Yeshua's supporters. He admonished them, "G_d is on our side. Not even mighty Rome can stand up to Him. The kingdom is in our midst!"

"We will secure the Temple at noon Thursday, open the Holy of Holies, and that night celebrate Pesah Shabbat free again. Freed like our ancestors were from Pharoah and Egypt, freed from Roman oppression and priestly apostasy. And weekly Shabbat will restore G-d's house as a house of prayer for all people."

Yehudah (Judas) had all he needed to know.

CHAPTER 22

Plots and plans revealed

Pilate, Antipas, and Caiaphas met as planned throughout the week. They all breathed a sign of relief when both cohorts arrived in Jerusalem and were stationed in the Antonia, the Praetorium, and around the Temple walls.

Wednesday evening he was back.

Demanding to see Caiaphas despite his momentary forgetfulness, Yehudah sent word that he was one of the Council and had spoken to Caiaphas earlier. He insisted that he had crucial information, urgent information and would not be turned away. Caiaphas relented with a threat and had him brought in.

"This had better be important; I'm already late for an engagement," he spouted with a tone of exasperation.

"Do you want to know when and where he will be without the presence of the mob?" Yehudah tempted with a slight snarl on his lips. The hook set, and Yehudah was sure he detected relief and immediate attention.

"What do you think? Give it to me man!"

"First I must be sure I'll be paid. I'm risking everything being here," Yehudah demanded.

"Of course. You have my word. Now tell me what I need to know."

With that assurance Yehudah restated the details of the conversation from earlier that afternoon. Caiaphas could hardly contain his excitement.

"We are scheduled to gather for dinner tomorrow in the home of Yaaqov, his brother. His house is..."

"Yes, yes. I know. In the lower city. We have had him under surveillance for sometime," Caiaphas interrupted him.

"Well, after the meal the plans are to retire to a secret garden in the Kidron, a garden where Yaaqov meets with followers from south Jerusalem and where Yeshua meets with them when he's in the city. I know where it is; I've been there numerous times. There might be a dozen of us, maybe two. They have started carrying swords. Early Yom Shishi morning Yeshua plans to gather everyone on the Mount of Olives and march to the Temple." Yehudah was prepared to go on with the details, but Caiaphas had had enough.

"We need to know when the group leaves Yaaqov's house and heads for the Kidron. The easiest way I can think of so as not to tip our hand or draw a crowd is for you to meet the soldiers and lead them to the spot. Temple Guards and Roman soldiers will already be south of the Temple around Herod's Porch. Their presence won't be suspicious. Can you get away from the group, find us, and lead the soldiers to the garden?"

"I can find some excuse but I don't want to be associated with the troops," Yehudah protested.

"You don't have a choice if you want to be paid. Besides in the dark and in a crowd, he has to be identified. Lead the soldiers to him and get lost."

"Alright, but I want my money."

With some calculation Caiaphas snarled, "Half now and half later. I want to be sure this isn't a set up, and you leazazel (damn) well better know if anything happens and we don't get him, I'll want my money back. We know where to find you."

"Get him 15 shekels," he ordered a servant.

"We'll be waiting tomorrow night," Caiaphas promised as he dismissed Yehudah with a wave of his hand.

Yehudah hadn't finished counting his blood money before Caiaphas was out the door and headed for the Palace to meet with Pilate and Antipas. Breathlessly he recounted his conversation with the disciple, unable to hide his pleasure. Pilate was pleased. It only remained for him to direct Caiaphas to have 50 of the Temple Guard on ready at Herod's Porch to accompany and support the Roman cohort.

Summoning the centurion, Pilate made it clear to his co-conspirators who was in charge.

"Petronius, tomorrow at 9th watch have your men assembled and battle ready below the south wall of the Temple. The Temple Guard will follow your orders. They are there only to show anyone that witnesses your action that I have the support of the Jewish authorities. Tolerate no interference. Force is usually sufficient to dispel cowards. Is that clear?"

"Yes my Lord." With a clear vision and unquestioned determinism, Petronius turned to prepare.

"Now that that's settled, I have just one question," Pilate said. "My motives are obvious. I will not tolerate sedition. We saw its ugly face in Galilee and when your father died, Antipas. Rome will not tolerate any threat to its rule. Any claims to kingship will be abolished, swiftly and without leniency."

"To be truthful," Caiaphas objected, "he hasn't exactly claimed to be a king, only to proclaim some coming kingdom, and he hasn't excited any violence."

"It's all the same to me. I have my justification. This rabble rouser will be eliminated. However, I'm not sure why you are so insistent that he be removed."

Antipas responded quickly. "I share your motives, Prefect. You are well aware that the Galilee has a history of political and social unrest. Tradition has it that a remnant of the Davidic line settled in Nazareth or Kochba, or somewhere in Galilee. The pernicious lies won't die. I am the recognized representative of Rome there. If anyone deserves the title 'King of the Jews,' like my father wore at Augustus' bequest, it is I, your loyal servant."

"That still doesn't tell me why you, Caiaphas, have such a passionate investment in this."

"My Lord, I serve at your favor. Your guards protect the raiments of my office and release them only on designated holy days. We priests have served since the days of Aaron, Nathan, and Josiah. My line was chosen when Pompey brought Israel under Roman 'protection.' From the beginning we have been charged with maintaining ritual observance, cultic purity, personal morality. This man has blatantly violated our Shabbat rules. He rubs our noses in his disregard for ritual purity. You saw what he did in the

Temple last Shabbat. That was not some innocent misdemeanor without meaning or significance. He has challenged the very heart and purpose of the Temple, and his followers multiply before your very eyes."

"Then," demanded Pilate, "why haven't you taken care of this yourselves before now? We've granted you certain jurisdiction and, albeit, authority."

"With all due respect, Dominus, we don't have the authority to do the one thing that will solve both your and our problem. Truthfully, my reasons don't deserve death; yours do. I would not protest such action on your part. You have cause; I am inconvenienced."

"Fortunately or unfortunately, you are right. And I am out of patience with this nuisance," Pilate concluded. "In two days this will all be behind us. Rest well gentlemen."

CHAPTER 23

Temple, treachery, together

Jerusalem awoke to a typical Pesah week Yom Chamishi. Personal hygiene, morning prayers, light breakfast (matzah, fruit, goat milk if lucky), Temple worship for pilgrims; residents had the added duties of commercial activities. Merchants looked forward to this festival because they would easily garner 25% on their annual income from this one week. Consequently they didn't want anything to disrupt that process.

Priests were especially anxious that crowds were controlled and orderly. The Torah obligation of Temple tax mainly depended on an individual's sense of moral duty and the uncertain ability to pay. And there were always the unscrupulous tax collectors who lined their pockets first and "doctored" the reports they sent to Jerusalem. In truth the Temple Treasurer knew that Rome got its 30-40% before anyone else saw a denarius.

This week the festival provided the unparalleled opportunity to extract the minimum "offering" and more, as pilgrims made their way into the sanctuary. The granary would swell to overflowing, and the Romans closely monitored the opulent Treasury with envy. Pilate filled his private coffers to the maximum possible without incurring the wrath of the Senate.

Up early as his habit had always been, after kissing Mariamne and a sleeping Yehuda, Yeshua found solitude in the hills outside Bethany. Wrapped in his tzitzit he quietly mouthed the Shema and, as his mother had taught him so long ago, prayed, "Abba, your will, your kingdom." Mariamne shared his passion and never interrupted his reverie.

Neither did he shorten his routine this morning. A calmness seemed to have settled over him in the last day or two. That calmness was not to be mistaken for resolve. Rather it was clarity of purpose and acceptance of the inevitable Day of the L–d. He and Mariamne were clear about his role; he was the agent, the messenger. YHWH was in control. He was servant; YHWH was L–d. He had walked the fine line between aggressive demands and aggressive action. Even with Yohanan's death, he avoided angry retaliation.

Those who had been with him from the beginning came to understand; others did not. Brother Yaaqov preserved the most faithful memory of his sermons. "Faith without works is dead." Time would distort message and meaning. People hear what they want or need to hear.

Today there was work to be done.

Today Yeshua insisted that Mariamne remain in Bethany. She and Yehuda would come to Temple tomorrow. Together with Yeshua and all Israel they would welcome the kingdom. Today he would confront the authorities with one last invitation.

He promised to return in the evening. In reassuring tones he shared his plan to spend the day in Temple. With everything that had to be done for Yom Shishi and the Shabbat, Yeshua knew a multitude of Sadducees and priests, not to mention the Sanhedren, would posture prominently for favor and recognition. He intended to challenge their arrogance and self-serving practices.

He and the Council needed one more evening to coordinate Yom Shishi's maneuvers and had agreed to meet at Yaaqov's house for the evening meal. It might take some time. Plus he wanted to reinforce to the followers in the Kidron and on Mount Olive the necessity to avoid confrontation with the Romans before noon on Yom Shishi. They were the most vulnerable within sight of Roman and Temple Guards. Therefore, he told Mariamne not to wait up for him. He promised to be by her side at dawn.

* * *

Accompanied by Shimon, Andrew, Yosa, and Philip, Yeshua turned his eyes toward Zion. Not unaware of its significance they boldly and brazenly strode through the Golden Gate just as he had done the previous Shabbat. The other disciples headed for their respective destinations, barely able to constrain their enthusiasm. A multitude takes discipline to control; a mob only responds to authority. They were determined not to let this get out of hand.

Yeshua had guessed well. Inside the walls the pompous hypocrites were easily spotted strutting around with their entourages. A loud voice, a pointing finger, a well placed accusation and he had a ready made audience.

"Vipers! Thieves! You go around with long faces, beating your breasts and giving thanks that you're not like all these other poor publicans. YHWH has turned a deaf ear to your hollow, self-righteous boasts. He will empty this house of its corruption and write a new covenant on the hearts of His righteous ones. How long do you think He will tolerate you compromising with the idolaters? How long do you think YHWH will go before He hears the cries of the oppressed, the widows, the orphans? How long do you think He will turn His back on the rape of His land and His people?

YHWH demands, yearns for justice and mercy and kindness. You had better get ready! This is the Year of the L–d. The Day of the L–d is at hand. The kingdom is coming, indeed has already broken in. <u>Now</u> is the acceptable Year of the L–d."

The level of their screams was only matched by the intensity of their anger. Yosa, in spite of his youth, sensed the danger and potential harm building and, without thinking, grabbed Yeshua pulling him into the anonymity of the crowd. Fortunately it worked, and soon the hysteria lost its object of scorn.

Retreating through the passage under the Royal Porch to the safety of the Pool of Siloam, Yeshua and the others enjoyed the coolness of the refreshing spring.

"I got carried away; I intended that message for tomorrow morning. They'll just have to hear it twice. Anyway, the seeds are sown. We'll have to see what kind of ground they fall on."

Realizing enough disruption had been generated for one day, the group decided to make their way to Yaaqov's house. Evening was approaching and the others were to start gathering. Sure enough, when they arrived everyone else but the "sons of thunder" and Thaddeus was there. The remainder were expected within the hour.

Yaaqov was quiet and introspective. Same father, same mother, but two brothers that were very different. Yaaqov was observant and pious. Yeshua could bend a rule when occasion necessitated. They both organized their day around prayer, but Yaaqov wanted to be near the Temple. He spent so much time there after moving to Jerusalem that he became known by face and name. That doesn't mean that he approved of everything that went on there. He didn't, but he didn't equate Temple with priests either. He yearned for covenant renewal and the coming kingdom. Right now he just left the preaching and confrontation to Yeshua. He knew Yeshua had a special mission; he was willing to be supportive. So here they were, and Yaaqov cast his lot with Yeshua.

Tomorrow, Yom Shishi evening, Shabbat and Pesah (Nisan 14) the Council would celebrate with all Israel in the kingdom, but tonight was business. Having ritually bathed face, hands, and feet they gathered around the table. Yaaqov had prepared a gracious and simple meal. Tonight was bread and wine and spring vegetables. Tomorrow lamb! Having discontinued the keeping of servants and deliberately disavowing ownership of a slave, Yaaqov like all the Council provided for themselves and shared household duties with spouses or in group homes or camps. Women contributed significantly to the financial support of the mission and accordingly shared in the decision making. Mariamne set the example.

The agenda was urgent, and time was precious. Before Yeshua's assault on the Court of Priests and the Holy Place at noon, the Council needed to be positioned in the Court of Israel. Yeshua insisted that the women have access as well. Orders were for them to cover their heads with tzitzits and, if challenged by Temple Guards at the entrance, men and women were to be tightly packed and forcibly press forward. The religious fervor of the Day should reduce the likelihood of anyone being excluded.

Coordination of entry and gate assignments were critical. All groups were to converge on their respective Temple Mount gates at the third hour. This meant rising at dawn, ritually preparing, and at least providing the small children with breakfast.

After Yeshua intoned the evening prayer, he designated each disciple's gate as they ate their meal.

"Shimon and Andrew, you are to bring your people up the stairs and through the Coponius Gate directly under the Roman Eagle. Shimon (the Zealot), you take the gate to the right of the Coponius Gate at the lower level. Philip and Nathaniel, take the stairs to and through the southwest corner tower where the porticoes meet Herod's Basilica. Brother Yaaqov, since you are already down here, you and Thaddeus enter through the left side Huldah Gate. This will bring you right up into the Court of the Gentiles. Matya and Thomas, bring your people from the Kidron and enter through the Huldah Gate on the right side. The streets are narrow and confusing in that area; so don't get lost and allow plenty of time to get there. You'll come up in the Court of the Gentiles also. Look for Yaaqov and Thaddeus and spread out once you get inside.

Yaaqov and Yohanan (sons of thunder), it's time to live up to your names (he said with a broad smile)! You bring your people through the north Portico Gate. It's big enough to accommodate a larger crowd. Spread out and you will be opposite those on the other side of the Court of the Gentiles."

"What about me? Have you forgotten me," asked Yehudah?

"Yehudah bar Iscariot, I've trusted you with so much for so long and saved you for another important duty. Young Yehuda (brother) is so eager and has learned well, but he needs mature guidance. I want you two to bring your groups through the lower gate left of Coponius Gate on the western side. Take your people to the left to join Yaaqov's and Yohanan's people in the upper half of the Court of the Gentiles.

"All of this should go smoothly and relatively unnoticed to this point. You'll pretty much blend in with all the other pilgrims. Now is when everything must come together precisely on cue. Once inside the Porticoes and stationed, send your designated runners to the Golden Gate.

"I will lead Mariamne, Yehuda, Yosa, and all the others from Bethany down the Mount of Olives through the Golden Gate. The meaning of my entry from the east will not be lost on the faithful. When the runners see us at the base of the Temple Mount, and only then, they are to return to each of you. It is imperative that you all immediately converge on the doors to the Court of the Women. Timing is everything.

"I have walked this route every day this week. I can do it blindfolded and know exactly how long it will take in this throng.

"As you enter make a passage straight through the Court of the Women, then the Court of Israel, and into the Court of Priests. Line both sides of the path.

"Shimon and Andrew, your group will be last before I arrive and by the time you are poised to enter, I will be there to follow you straight through to the stairs of the Holy Place. Instead of Caiaphas slaughtering the pascal lamb, I will proclaim the Day of the L–d and YHWH's kingdom will begin!"

With a slight quiver in his voice, Yehudah bar Iscariot asked, "what about the Romans and the Temple Guard?"

Yeshua retorted confidently, "I am only the moshiach; the battle is YHWH's"

Silently they each searched the faces of the others around the table. They drank deeply from the strength from Yeshua's calmness, and one after another raised their cups in unity and commitment.

No one heard the words spoken, but Yehudah leaned close to Yeshua. When he nodded in response, Yehudah quietly rose and started for the door. He paused long enough to hear Yeshua announce, "It's getting late. You need your rest. Shimon, Andrew, Yaaqov and Yohanan, brother Yaaqov, walk with me to the Kidron camp. I need your advice on a couple of matters."

Yehudah knew exactly where they were headed; he had been there numerous times over the last year. "I couldn't have scripted this better," he mused as he walked briskly through the darkening streets on his way to rendezvous with Caiaphas. "Now I know when, where, and how many. I'll get my money and all this foolishness will be over."

CHAPTER 24

Plans thwarted, relationships renewed

"Where in Gehenna have you been? We've been waiting over an hour."

Caiaphas had been more than on edge all day. Since before his marriage to Sarai, he lived in the shadow of Annas. A strong, powerful, and influential man, he had served as High Priest, but all high priests served at the behest of the Roman overlords. When he butted heads with Prefect Coponius, Annas was demoted. His revenge was to work behind the scenes and get his son-in-law, Caiaphas, appointed. Consequently Caiaphas had never been his own man. Despite all the intrigue, his natural talents secured for himself the longest tenure as High Priest of anyone in the Roman period. His role in this festival's episode was no small contribution.

This was his chance to demonstrate his value to Pilate and show some independence of thought and action. He consciously left Annas out of the loop as he plotted with Pilate and Antipas. He surprised Annas with a fait accompli.

Yehudah saw the light from the torches before he emerged from the ally south of Herod's Basilica. He surmised it was a substantial crowd, more than he had been led to believe would be available and more than he believed would be necessary. Climbing the stairs to where he saw Caiaphas surrounded by the Guard, he blurted out, "Why so many? I told you his entourage was small."

"I'm taking no chances. He will learn where power resides. What do you care anyway? It's out of your hands. This is Petronius; he's in charge from here. Take him to this 'Yeshua' and get lost. He has the remainder of your money once he is bound and secured."

Yehudah knew it was indeed out of his hands. There was no turning back even if he had wanted to. If Yeshua was the moshiach, YHWH would protect him. If not, he wanted his money and to get on with his life. Three years was long enough to wait.

"When you have him in chains, return him to me at my house. Don't keep me waiting long," Caiaphas instructed Petronius. Pushing Yehudah ahead down the steps, Petronius, the Temple Guard, and the Roman cohort hastened to the night's assignment.

"How will I know which one is your rabbi?" the Roman snarled.

Yehudah replied, "Stay close to me. When I find him I'll call his name and embrace him."

"This better not be some wild chase you're taking us on or you'll be the one chained and flogged."

Yehudah was quiet the rest of the way.

It was a little over half a mile from Herod's Basilica to the Kidron camp. Yehudah knew that leaving Yaaqov's house approximately when he did, they should arrive soon at the camp, if they weren't already there. He didn't want to risk missing them and still maintain the element of surprise, so he walked quickly through the old city, crossed the wall taking the path to the Gihon Spring, and headed for the Kidron camp.

Yeshua and the hand-picked few had indeed left the supper on the heels of Yehudah's departure. Unlike Yehudah and his party, they had taken the road passed the Pool of Siloam, crossed the city wall, and headed up the valley to the camp. Matya and Thomas had spent the week here in the south, gathering followers and preparing them for Yom Shishi. The two parties converged on the camp simultaneously. Yehudah preserved his element of surprise.

Several in the camp, realizing one of the groups was armed guards and soldiers, beat a hasty retreat into the surrounding darkness. Recognizing Yehudah at the head of the cohort, Yeshua was initially confused and froze in his tracks. Before he could think fast enough to ask Yehudah what he was doing there and why the soldiers, his disciple embraced him and kissed him. Even Petronius wasn't quite ready for the encounter. His hesitation allowed Yeshua time to regain composure.

"Who are you looking for?" he demanded.

Petronius, equally composed, responded, "Yeshua of Nazareth."

"That's me. What do you want?"

With that admission Petronius raised his sword and commanded two guards to seize him. Before they could obey, Shimon, Thomas, and Shimon the Zealot who had come along as well, drew their swords, swords they had not been ready to surrender yet, and stepped between them and Yeshua.

Swinging wildly like untrained pedestrians, they managed to wound three of the soldiers, one on the head and two on the arms, before they were subdued by the disciplined front line. By now Yeshua had stepped forward and shielding the others, ordered his followers to back away. Fear? Strategy? Rational assessment?

Petronius grasped the advantage of his superior numbers, superiority intended in case of a situation like this, and ordered his men to hold their positions. Once the two guards were instructed to finish their assignments, attention was taken away from the Galileans on the ground, and they managed to slip into the faceless spectators and avoid arrest themselves. Petronius' assignment was specific. Cut off the head and the serpent will die. He chose not to risk losing the lives of any under his command and, not knowing how many if any others were armed, he decided to take his quarry and return to Caiaphas. Finding Yehudah quaking in the shadows, he threw the money pouch at him and turned on his heel.

Petronius warned the remaining stragglers to disperse and not show up at the Temple the next day. The soldiers bound Yeshua tightly, maybe a little too much so and placed him in the middle of the cohort where no one could get near him. They retraced their steps by the Gihon, across the wall, and passed the Judgment Seat on the steps of the Basilica to Caiaphas' house.

It was approaching midnight. A company that large does not move quietly, even if they want to and Petronius didn't care. Several residents woke but chose not to get involved. The Romans were too focused on the job at hand to notice, some safe distance behind and always cloaked in darkness, two men followed to see where they were taking Yeshua.

When they arrived at the High Priest's house, they knocked on the gate and were admitted to the inner courtyard where a hand full of servants warmed themselves around a small fire. Petronius and the two guards who had bound Yeshua were escorted into the house and up stairs to the central hall. The balcony to the hall overlooked the courtyard, and by the time they had gotten upstairs, two more figures merged with the servants around the fire. Caiaphas came down from the family quarters to the central hall.

Yaaqov had never been inside Caiaphas' house. He had known him from Capernaum years ago and observed his rise to power; there had been no communication between them since those early years. His daily presence at the Temple earned him respect and recognition. One of the Temple Guard he befriended during that time vouched for him and permitted entrance minutes before. Shimon simply followed him without uttering a word. From the courtyard below they heard the conversation grow more heated.

"So, Yeshua of Nazareth, we meet again. Do you have any idea who I am?" Caiaphas queried.

"Of course I do, Caiaphas. How can I forget someone who saved my life! You've done well for yourself. Too bad you've neglected the one thing that matters most."

"You insolent mamzer! I see you haven't changed. Do you have any idea the harah you're in? As if it's not enough that you ignore ritual purification and Shabbat regulations, you put yourself on a level with G-d claiming to speak for Him."

"Stop right there. It's time you got your facts straight. I do not deny that I am not a slave to Shabbat. At creation G-d gave Shabbat to us; He didn't give us to Shabbat. I do not and have never claimed equality with G-d. I know as well as you the blasphemy of such insanity. But I do claim to speak for Adonai. I am His messenger to a vile and corrupt generation. You strut around Jerusalem, self-absorbed, clueless as to what G-d requires of us. You line your pockets with gold and silver while the sons and daughters of Israel go hungry, lose their land, become destitute and homeless. If you knew the Law and the Prophets, you'd be on your knees begging for forgiveness."

"Leazazel enough! I might not be able to get rid of you and the rabble that hang on your every word, but I know someone who can't wait to get his hands on you. I can't believe I thought I could talk some sense into that thick skull of yours. I remember a young girl you were fond of. I promise you she'll regret the day you met."

Defensively Yeshua responded, "Leave her and the boy out of this..." and immediately regretted his angry words.

"Oh, this is even better than I hoped. Let's see how sure and self-righteous you are this time tomorrow," Caiaphas interrupted him gleefully.

Turning to Petronius the High Priest ordered, "Take him to the praetorian and 'soften' him up for the Prefect. Pilate was very specific that you wake him at dawn so he can take care of this matter early. Put your men on alert just in case some of these idiots decide to do something stupid and have your men there to encourage him to demonstrate a little Roman justice. These people need to be taught a lesson."

Yaaqov and Shimon heard all they needed and quickly slipped out into the darkness. "I'll let Andrew, Yehudah, Yaaqov and Yohanan, and the people in Bethany know what has happened. You get to Shimon the Zealot, Philip, Nathaniel, Matya, and Thomas. They must be stopped. Without Yeshua there's nothing. I can't believe this—first Yohanan the Baptizer and now Yeshua," Shimon whispered breathlessly.

Grabbing his arm Yaaqov spoke with authority, "It won't be safe to be seen in public for a couple of days. Tell the Council to gather at my house as quickly as possible. If the Romans had wanted more of us, they would have arrested us earlier in the Kidron. We don't need to tempt them. Now hurry."

CHAPTER 25

Day of Preparation

Drunk soldiers can be cruel, especially Jew-haters with an extra ration of wine under their belts. Their worst torture was reserved for political prisoners, and they seemed to revel taking someone as close to death for as long as possible. The public spectacle satisfied their basest instincts and very effectively discouraged oppressed populations from any thoughts of rebellion.

While Pilate slept, the garrison in the praetorian engaged in some extra-curricular activity. Metal-studded straps, needled whips, and thorn boughs were effective. Deep in the bowels of the fort, screams of pain fell on deaf ears of the sleeping city. Vinegar poured over raw flesh heightened the sensitivity.

As instructed, Petronius had the Prefect awakened precisely at dawn. The centurion was into his second day without sleep. The Prefect was irritable from a short night of restless dreaming.

"Dominus, the Jewish pretender is in the praetorian awaiting you. If it's any consolation, he didn't get any sleep last night," he reported with a sinister smile on his lips. By this point he was running on adrenaline and oblivious to his body's craving for rest.

Without breakfast, Pilate left the Royal Palace and made the short walk to Gabbatha by which time Petronius was waiting with the prisoner. But not only Petronius. The night's activity had disturbed many of the city's inhabitants. Several pilgrims in the surrounding camps were alarmed by warnings carried by Yaaqov and Shimon. A crowd of two to three hundred found Gabbatha and were nervous and anxious to learn what Pilate and the Romans would do.

Other followers of Yeshua, less dedicated to the campaign, were already leaving Jerusalem and abandoning their "messianic" leader. It is easy to shout "hosanna" without a Roman spear pointed at your chest.

Ignoring advice to the contrary, Mariamne and Mary left Yehuda in the care of Mary and Martha and went into the city. They didn't find him until after the execution had begun.

After seating himself in the Judgment Seat, Pilate surveyed the gathering. Guards drug Yeshua in front of the dais and threw him to the ground. He was a crumpled mass of naked, bleeding flesh. Death was inevitable regardless of the pending horror.

"So, this is the King of the Jews! What have you got to say for yourself, oh Great King?" Yeshua remained silent.

"Put him on his feet," Pilate barked. "Look at me Jew. Where is your army now? What kingdom do you rule, dog?"

The night's abuse had broken more than one rib and his right eye was blinded by the thorns they had wrapped around his head in amusement. With pain and difficulty Yeshua drew a tortured breath and whispered, "My father's kingdom is not this corrupt world."

"Talk louder. I can't hear you," he bellowed.

With all the strength he could muster, the Galilean replied, "My father's kingdom is love and peace, not swords and war. I am only the messenger; His army will wipe you from the face of this earth and free Israel once and for all. You and Rome will not stand in the judgment."

Pilate grew angrier with each word. He pounded his fist on the table beside him, knocking over the wine vessel and breaking the cup. As he leaped to his feet he demanded, "Where is your father? Are there others? Where are your cohorts?" But Yeshua was too exhausted to answer if he had wanted to.

In the face of this insolence, Pilate turned to Petronius and proclaimed, "Take him to Golgatha immediately and crucify him. Use the nails, not the ropes. Make a sign that says 'King of the Jews' and put it over his head. I'll show this worthless, backwater, latrine of a country what happens when you even <u>pretend</u> to challenge Rome. Just for good measure take the two lestai being held in the Antonia Fortress that the Temple Guard arrested earlier this week and crucify them with this piece of harah. I want all Jerusalem to see the consequence of this debacle." Turning on his heel, the Prefect left them with the responsibility to carry out his orders.

And they did within the hour.

CHAPTER 26

Roman justice: death and burial

Mariamne and Mary took the road from Bethany north through the Kidron. Just north of the Temple they chose the road into the city into a section known as Bezetha. Now they were lost, but fortunately Yaaqov accompanied them. When they insisted on trying to find Yeshua, he refused to let them travel alone. "Far too risky," he said.

It wasn't the most familiar part of Jerusalem to him, but Yaaqov knew that if he kept the Antonia Fortress and Herod's wall on his left, he would eventually find the Royal Palace. Street rumors were only partially right. Walking as fast as possible, Mary was older and doing the best she could; they sensed tension in the air and heard occasional comments about something going on at Golgatha. Realizing that several people were making their way in that direction, these faithful, frightened three decided to follow.

They heard the anguished cries before they saw the hill. Leaving the wall behind them and turning north, they soon saw three crosses silhouetted against the morning sky. Inhuman cries of pain pierced their hearts.

* * *

Petronius dispatched a dozen soldiers to retrieve the two lestai and meet them at Golgatha. A place not infrequently used for brutal exhibitions, the hill was dotted with crosses and poles from previous executions. They were reusable so trees were saved in the process. The only decision was which to use, cross beams with nails or ropes or spiked poles for simple impalements. At Pilate's preference the centurion chose the cross beam for Yeshua since death would come slower. The lestai got spikes to satisfy the guards' thirst for agony despite the brevity.

Naked, bloody, and filthy with his own defecation, torture does not include time for privacy or personal hygiene, Yeshua was thrown prostrate on the ground beside the chosen instrument. He got to wait and watch, and hear the pleas and dieing screams of the other men. Once they were impaled on upright poles, they were left writhing in pain and begging for death. Now it was his turn.

There was not an ounce of strength remaining in him. Unable to resist, they straddled him over a short, supportive protrusion, drove a nail through each wrist into the cross beam, and placing his feet on each side of the upright, they drove nails through his ankles. To insure that the victim could not free a foot, they bent the nail head securely against the bone. Yeshua's screams only incited his executioners. Lifting the cross and placing it in the hole to hold it only heightened the agony of someone attached only with nails. Petronius was left with the final irony of tying a crude sign over his head before the pole was raised. As instructed, it read "Yeshua of Nazareth–King of the Jews."

The three arrived after the work was completed. While guards sat, joked, and drank, waiting for death so they could dispose of the bodies and return to the barracks, the Jews who bothered to witness the horror did so quickly and departed. Whether they knew the victims or not, they remembered the Torah and shared the shame. "Cursed is he who hangs on a tree."

Cautiously and longingly Mariamne, Mary, and Yaaqov climbed the hill and approached the cross. The centurion, leaning on his spear for much needed rest, deliberately stepped in front of them with an out-stretched arm. "Halt. Stay away or you'll share his fate."

Without hesitating Mary said, "I'm his mother." Drawing on her courage, Mariamne said, "I'm his wife." Petronius thought he recognized Yaaqov but did not sense any danger. Tired or just repulsed by the day's events, he acquiesced. "Alright, but make it quick."

The women sobbed uncontrollably and caressed his bleeding feet. Yaaqov stood silently staring into his brother's face. Numbed by hours of pain and loss of blood, Yeshua managed a faint smile of recognition.

"I love you with all my heart Mariamne. Tell Yehuda his father loves him." It was a few minutes before he spoke again.

When he spoke his voice was weaker. "Mother, where is G-d? I did what He asked."

Silent again, he finally addressed Yaaqov last. "Beloved brother. Now you are head of the family. Take care of them. Remember."

They heard the gurgling as his lungs filled with blood. Despite the prolonged beating and nails in his wrists and ankles, he died from lack of air. No longer able to hold himself up, his head slumped and his diaphragm collapsed. He quietly suffocated.

"Back off," the centurion ordered. "Leave."

As they walked down the hill away from the crest Yaaqov turned and asked, "What will you do with the bodies?"

"What we always do, throw them to the dogs!"

Thinking quickly, Yaaqov implored, "Please sire let us have him. There are some burial tombs near here. We'll take him and you won't have to bother with him."

Petronius didn't seem to be listening. The guards had already just about finished their job. That usually meant breaking the legs of the victims just to be sure they were dead. They had done this to the lestai and taken them off the poles, throwing one on top of the other. As they approached the last man the centurion stopped them.

"He's dead, but one last jab won't hurt." And with that he thrust his spear into Yeshua's side. As expected, no response. Turning to the three he said, almost reluctantly, "I can't let you have him. It's against protocol. Now beat it before I have to do something unpleasant."

Disappointed, they continued down the hill. Yaaqov wrapped his arms around them tenderly and spoke softly, "Once they can't see us anymore, you two be careful and watch what they do with the bodies. I'm going to get Thaddeus and we'll be back as soon as possible. What they don't know won't hurt them. We'll take Yeshua and give him a proper burial. What do they care about one more dead Jew."

*   *   *

This day was like any other to Pilate. A Day of Preparation meant nothing to him. Pesah was a nuisance. He much preferred his residence in Caesaria Maritima and the entertainments that awaited him there. All he wanted was to get through this week as quickly and quietly as possible.

Now that the business of the morning was over, Petronius reported the successful completion of the execution with desired effect on a subdued population. The Prefect ate his lunch and anticipated a relaxing evening. He knew every Jew in Jerusalem would be at home with family eating some commemorative meal he never fully understood or appreciated. What he did understand was that tomorrow was Shabbat to the Jews, and he could enjoy a restful day.

*   *   *

Herod Antipas chose not to provoke his Jewish subjects this weekend. He avoided any public appearance with the Roman overlords. He stood in full regalia in the Court of Israel at the entrance to the Court of Priests. From his station he watched as the High Priest approached the altar. Two priests held the sacrificial lamb as Caiaphas raised the ritual blade. Precisely at noon he slit the paschal lamb's throat, spilling its blood on the altar for the people's sins and in remembrance of that night long ago when the Hebrews prepared to escape from Egypt.

A deafening cry went up from the people first in the Court of Israel, then the Women's Court, and then throughout the Court of the Gentiles.

Herod returned to his palace and settled in for a quiet seder and reflective Shabbat. But he couldn't shake an uneasy feeling that had troubled him for the week. Any messianic would-be had to be terminated. He was the legitimate "King of the Jews" if he could just get Tiberius to give him the title. Pilate's insult did not sit well. What else could he do? After all he had built and named a city after the emperor.

But it still bothered him that Romans continued to slaughter Jewish citizens, rightly or wrongly.

*   *   *

Caiaphas was more than happy to turn the Nazarean over to the Prefect. He had regretted ever knowing him practically from the beginning. If he just hadn't been at the shore that day long ago! And besides, despite his own illicit fantasies, he had to admit his jealousy. This peasant enjoyed pleasures he was forbidden. He had never forgotten her.

After finishing the interrogation last night, he got what little sleep was possible and rose early. Every eye in Jerusalem would be on him today. His morning mikvah and light breakfast completed, he departed for the Temple.

First he went by the Antonia Fortress to get his vestments for this day (held in captivity by the Romans) and then to the High Priest's private chambers in the Temple to prepare for the Day's climactic event. His aids were waiting for him.

While ceremonial, he still felt a tingle as he stepped toward the altar, intoned the prayer, and raised the blade. In spite of the solemnity of the occasion, Yeshua had not left his thoughts from the moment he opened his eyes.

"Can I forget the man and listen to the message? I know it's a sabbatical year. I hate the Romans too and long for freedom. But who am I; who are we to stand up to them, the greatest empire the world has known? I saw what they did to Yehudah the Galilean; I know what they did to Archelaus. War would be suicide. He and those like him have to die so we can live!"

That thought gave him extra strength as he thrust the blade through the lamb's throat. In his eyes, the lamb was Yeshua.

Even seder and Pesah denied him rest. Alarming reports of a stolen body and groups of followers continuing to live according to his teaching claiming he was coming back to initiate G-d's kingdom on earth gave him nightmares for years.

"Is there no end to this pernicious lie?"

* * *

Yaaqov ran as fast as he could by the Royal Palace, through the narrow streets and alleys to his house. He had told Thaddeus he would return and expected to find him there. He was.

"They killed him," he gasped breathlessly, "and they are desecrating his body. I need your help."

"What can we do?"

"We can get his body and bury it properly, but it won't be easy. They just threw the bodies in a heap."

"What bodies?" Thaddeus asked. "What happened?"

"They beat him all night and then in the early morning, they crucified him along with two other men I don't know."

"Oh G-d. Oh G-d."

"Go next door and borrow Eleazer's ass. Tell him we'll bring it back tomorrow. I'll get some sheets. Mother and Mariamne are waiting at Golgatha to show us where they placed him," Yaaqov told him.

"Is there time? We hardly have two hours before Shabbat begins and tonight is Pesah seder."

"We have to hurry, but we can do this. Go and meet me out front."

They retraced Yaaqov's earlier route trying to be as inconspicuous as possible. Two men with an ass and a load on its back got little attention. Jerusalem was too preoccupied with Pesah preparation. Reaching Golgatha the men did not see the women anywhere. Yaaqov almost panicked as time was running out. "Work" and handling a dead body makes you ritually impure on Shabbat. They had to complete the burial and cleanse themselves.

At that moment Mariamne came running from behind some rocks on the western side of the hill. "Be careful. The guards have left but there are a couple of stragglers hanging around."

Thaddeus and Yaaqov followed her to where Mary waited, watching to be sure nothing happened to the body. "We can't wait. They'll have to assume we're family and taking him for burial."

The four went to where the bodies had been thrown down a ravine. It was too steep for the ass so Yaaqov and Thaddeus took the sheets and slid down to the mutilated remains. Almost overcome by the stench of death, they wrapped their noses and mouths with their shawls, spread the sheets on the ground, and went to get the body. It was not immediately clear which one was Yeshua.

Yaaqov reverently rolled the top body over on its side. It wasn't he. He was the second one in the pile. With some difficulty Yaaqov recognized his brother and the tears came again. Motioning to Thaddeus, they took him by the hands and feet and placed him on the top sheet. After crossing his arms over his chest, they wrapped him first in the top sheet and then in the second one so the body was completely covered and, hopefully, without suspicion.

It took some effort for the two men to get the body up the incline, but once they did they placed it on the animal to look like any ordinary burden.

"What now? Where do we take him?" Mary asked through her sorrow.

"I purchased a cave in the Talpiot district last year when Elizabeth died. There are several burial sites there," Yaaqov answered. The women remembered but they had been north in Magdala and did not learn of her death until a week later. By then she had been buried as required by Torah. "We can put him there; it's for the family. We must hurry before sunset or they decide to return."

They worked their way back south. Fortunately no one bothered them, and they reached the Talpiot cave before the sun dropped below the horizon. The men carefully removed the body from the ass' back, and after the women took down the temporary barrier to the opening, they took him inside the cave. Without a torch they could hardly see. Mariamne detected Elizabeth's body stretched out on a loculus to the right of the entrance.

"We don't have any more time. Let's leave him here for now. We'll come back after Shabbat with lime and spices and properly bathe and prepare the body. There's another loculus where we can lay him for the necessary time. By then I'll have an ossuary made for his bones."

Exiting the cave, Yaaqov and Thaddeus replaced the make shift covering. "After we finish kodesh I'll find a stone to cover the opening more permanently."

Mariamne noticed the chevron carved in the rock but chose not to inquire about it. As Yaaqov turned to go, Mariamne pleaded, "Come with us to Bethany. I'm sure Mary and Martha are anxious to hear what happened today and to know that we are alright. They'll expect us for seder and besides, without Elizabeth, you need to be with our family tonight. My heart's breaking to be with Yehuda ."

Silently Yaaqov accepted the hospitality that was their hallmark.

CHAPTER 27

Pesah, burial, and beyond

"Look what cousin Lazarus made for me," Yehuda exclaimed gleefully when he saw his mother. Only six years old, he didn't comprehend the seriousness of the day's events, neither did he know of his father's death. Mariamne took him in her arms and sobbed quietly. The siblings needed no words to confirm their worst fears.

Rumors spread throughout the city and surrounding villages all day. Hoping against hope they clung to the thinnest thread that Yeshua was alive. Despair did not mask the relief on their faces when they saw the women and Yaaqov.

Yaaqov began with last night's events; Mariamne picked up the details at Golgatha, and Mary finished the narrative when her daughter-in-law could not continue. Lazarus shared with them the news that Shimon had come by about mid-afternoon. He told them that various Council members had decided it best to leave Jerusalem for awhile, maybe a month. Philip and Andrew had already left for Bethsaida, Nathaniel for Cana. Shimon the Zealot was on the way to the camp at Wadi Cherith. The "sons of thunder" were headed for Magdala to warn the community there while Matya and

Thomas were to rendezvous with Shimon at Aenon. For the moment safety took precedence over festival.

Catching them by surprise Yosa came bounding into the house. He went straight to his mother and threw his arms around her neck. "I didn't know where you went; I've been everywhere looking for you." Relieved to hold her son, Mary suddenly realized, "Where is your brother Yehudah?"

They looked at each other. In the excitement and uncertainty of the day, no one took responsibility to account for everyone. "I thought he was with you." "I thought he was with you." "Did Shimon not mention him?"

"Wait, didn't Yeshua tell him to assist Yehudah bar Iscariot with the followers at the gate left of Coponius Gate?" remembered Yaaqov. "Has anyone seen either of them?"

They all shook their heads, and their sorrow was only compounded with another son/brother missing.

It fell to Yaaqov at last to say, "Hear, O Israel; the L–d our G–d is one L–d; and you shall love the L–d your G–d with all your heart, and with all your soul, and with all your might. Yeshua intended to celebrate Pesah tonight. I think we should in his memory and in hope of deliverance."

They gathered around the table Mary and Martha had prepared.

*　*　*

Shabbat was restricted to home sitting shiva, praying the kodesh, reciting scripture.

Early on Yom Rishon Yaaqov, Thaddeus, Mary, and Mariamne departed Bethany to return to Talpiot. Mariamne left Yehuda sleeping. "He'll be fine here. Hurry back," Martha offered.

"You three go to the tomb and start preparing the body. I'll get the spices, lime, and cloth we'll need for final burial and meet you there as soon as I can," Yaaqov directed. Once inside the city walls they parted ways to their respective tasks. Yaaqov headed for his house to get the denarii necessary to purchase the spices.

Entering the courtyard he was baffled. There propped at the door was a bag of myrrh, at least a hundred pounds of lime, and a brand new burial shroud. No note identified the giver, no explanation. Who knew that would do something like this? Who knew where he lived or that he had the body?

With some effort he gathered up everything, put it over his shoulder, and started for the cave. He arrived just as the three cleared the entrance. "We didn't expect you as soon. Here let me help you with that."

Yaaqov described the mystery that was waiting for him at the house. They too were at a loss to imagine who might have done such a thing. But there were more important things to tend to now.

Once their eyes grew accustomed to the interior, they silently immersed themselves in the sacred ritual. Tenderly mother and wife washed the body that was bloated with death and beginning to smell. Mariamne gently fingered each scar from head and face to shoulders and wrists, from back to side and thighs to ankles. Memory of nights of love flooded her mind, nights she knew were not to be repeated.

Thaddeus cleared the central cave of dust and rocks. Yaaqov draped the sheet over the loculus leaving a loose half for overlay and spread a layer of lime where the body would be placed. As the women worked their way down the body Thaddeus propped Yeshua while Yaaqov rubbed him with spices and wrapped him with cloth strips. Thaddeus held his head and shoulders to keep the body from touching the soiled sheet. Mariamne held his hips, and when finished Mary held his feet until Yaaqov could take him. After the men carefully laid him on the clean sheet, Mariamne caressed Yeshua's body one last time with the remaining spices. Yaaqov applied one more layer of lime and, after the women tucked the loose half over the body under his head and feet, Yaaqov scooped the remainder of the lime over the sheet.

Reluctantly and after a prayer, the four withdrew from the cave and the men thoroughly concealed the opening. "I'll put a stone there after his bones are in an ossuary." There would be two more bodies in the tomb before then.

"Mother, he wanted you with me. Not only is it my duty, but you know I want you to live with me. You and Yehuda as well, Mariamne. We know my Levirate responsibility, but you and I are probably beyond that. We have work to do."

"I need to collect my few things from the Magdala house," Mary replied, grateful for her second son's strength.

The widow intoned, "Your generosity is boundless, but Yeshua wanted me in Galilee providing for the Poor there. We both have work to do, but yours is here, mine is where we began." He nodded. "The boy must learn and share his father's legacy. We'll be back."

Epilogue

Pontius Pilate served as Prefect of Judea from 26-36 CE. He was cruel, ruthless, and generally inept. Consequently Rome replaced him and verifiable information thereafter is absent. The one piece of non-biblical evidence about Pilate is an engraved stone found at Caesarea Maritima that conclusively labels him as a "Prefect." All four canonical New Testament gospels ascribe responsibility for the crucifixion of Jesus of Nazareth to him, making the execution the result of sedition and rebellion. Conversations in the Gospels, certainly with his wife, are purely fictional.

Herod Antipas ruled Galilee and Perea beginning in 4 BCE at the death of his father Herod the Great and until 39 CE when Caligula exiled him to Gaul. According to the Christian New Testament he was responsible for the beheading of John the Baptizer and involved in the decision to execute Jesus. The latter is unsubstantiated, the former generally accepted. He is a central participant in the Passion narrative in the non-canonical Gospel of Peter.

Caiaphas (Yehosef bar Kayafa) served as High Priest in Jerusalem from 18-36 CE. He was the son-in-law of Annas, a former high priest whose sons served in the post before and after Caiaphas. Caiaphas was removed from office approximately the same time Pilate was. A Sadducee, he would have opposed any political activity of the Zealots and apocalyptic "prophets" and, probably, would have cooperated with the Roman overlords. A brother-in-law, Annas II, was High Priest when James (Yaaqov), the brother of Jesus was executed by stoning in 62 CE. Annas II was removed from office by Agrippa II specifically for his support of the death of James. This connection further heightens the suspicion about animosity between the two families.

In November 1990 the family tomb of High Priest Caiaphas was discovered. It contained a decorated ossuary inscribed "Yehosef bar Qafa." Excavations after the 1967 Six Day War uncovered a mansion with a stone weight and inscription "Bar Kathros" in Aramaic. We have physical evidence of the existence of the man who encouraged the execution of Jesus.

Zealots eventually initiated the Jewish War of 67-73 CE. Gentile followers of Jesus fled to Pella, Jewish followers' loyalties were split, Sadducees would disappear without a Temple, and two Jewish sects survived: Rabbinic Judaism and Christianity.

When the Synoptic Gospels' list of the Council of Twelve are combined, the names fall into three groups of four each. The first four are always together and prominent. They are Simon (Peter), Andrew, James, and John. The last two are called "sons of thunder." The second set includes Philip, Bartholomew (perhaps confused with or double named Nathaniel), Matthew, and Thomas. Matthew is also called Levi and identified as "of Alphaeus" (Greek for Clophas the brother of Joseph who is known in the Gospel of John as the father of Jesus and first husband of Mary). Thomas means "twin," but whose twin (Jesus or Jude?) is uncertain. The last set includes James of Alpheus (note above), Jude ("of James" which here means "brother of James") and confused with Thaddeus, Simon the Zealot (an identification not to be taken lightly), and Judas Iscariot. At the least, five (James of Joseph, Jude, Simon the Zealot, Matthew, and James of Clophas) are Jesus' brothers and half-brothers, maybe a sixth (Thomas).

In 1953 excavations at the church at Dominus Flevit on the Mount of Olives unearthed what one scholar labeled a "Judeo-Christian necropolis." One ossuary discovered was clearly marked with the name Shimon bar Jonah and was identified by Father Bellarmino Bagatti. This is Simon Peter's name in the New Testament. While the Vatican claims to preserve this disciple's bones in the Basilica in Rome, archaeological work has failed to uncover any evidence of a Christian burial site there to date. Strictly legend associates Simon Peter with Rome. The New Testament is a much more reliable source for restricting the remainder of his life to Jerusalem in service to the "people of the Way" and representing James as needed in places like Antioch. In either case he was not the author of the canonical I and II Peter or the non-canonical Gospel of Peter.

Various traditions about the Twelve are too numerous and too legendary to include here.

Remaining personae requiring mention include:

Judas Iscariot figures prominently in the New Testament gospels although he is not mentioned in the writing of Paul the Apostle. He is named as the author of the pseudonymous second century Gospel of Judas, a claim obviously false. He has been the brunt of jokes, curses, and praise for almost twenty centuries. Yet we know absolutely nothing about him.

The two accounts of his death in the New Testament are so contradictory and ludicrous as to be entirely unreliable.

As a side note, the family tomb of Simon of Cyrene was discovered in 1941 in the Kidron Valley. It contained an ossuary with his name inscribed on the side. It is in the warehouse at the Hebrew University in Jerusalem today.

Mark 6:3 includes a James in the inventory of Jesus' siblings. He plays a very insignificant role in the Synoptics. More of him in a moment.

If one did not know the connection between Joseph and Clophas/ Alphaeus, James of Alphaeus' place in the Council would be minimized. James of Alphaeus was Jesus' half-brother.

After Jesus' death James bar Joseph became leader of the community of followers in Jerusalem. His is the controlling voice of decision at the Jerusalem Council in Acts 15 where he represents and demands "Jewish" ethical standards for Gentile converts to the Way. He is the pillar the Apostle Paul ridicules in his letter to the Galatians. This James is the primary resource for the canonical Epistle of James in which is preserved the most extensive body of Jesus' authentic words. James spent the rest of his life in Jerusalem as head of the Ebionites (Jewish Christians) and died a martyr to that cause in 62 CE.

A careful reading of the list of bishops of the Jerusalem church will conclusively demonstrate the continuation of the Jesus family dynasty, albeit ending in the second century CE.

This brings us to the Talpiot tomb.

Discovered in 1980 during the construction of an apartment complex, the East Talpiot tomb is in lower or southern Jerusalem. Easter morning March 30, 1980 Eliot Braun drove Yosef Gat to the site. They were joined by Amos Kloner and Shimon Gibson. Three of the chamber walls had two burial niches each. The southwest niche contained two ossuaries, the northwest niche two. From here going clockwise the next niche was empty, the next contained one ossuary, the next two, and the last three. There were three skulls and various bones scattered on the ground around the entrance chamber, duly noted as highly unusual. Over the cave/tomb entrance was an inverted V (Λ) enclosing a circle (O) or wreath (?).

The ten ossuaries were catalogued 80/500-509, removed from the tomb, and then photographed. Only the photo of the entrance was clear enough to be preserved. Skulls and bones were emptied from the ossuaries for further study and proper burial by religious authorities. Six of the ten had inscriptions on them.

Shimon Gibson made the official measurements and drawings of the tomb with all objects in their original locations.

Ossuary IAA: 80/509 vanished before it was photographed but **not** before it was catalogued. The importance and impact of this will be seen shortly. An apartment complex was constructed over the tomb in 1981.

The first critical moment and suspicious event came in 1994 when the official catalogue listed only nine ossuaries from the tomb.

The following year (1995) a BBC/CTVC British film crew went to Jerusalem to do a piece on "ossuaries." When shown the ossuaries in the IAA warehouse, there were only nine and only five had inscriptions. The story aired in 1996.

During the two hour presentation Amos Kloner was interviewed. He had written the official report of the excavation. He disregarded the names on the bone boxes as common and refused to acknowledge the significance of the name cluster. He gave only five minutes to a discussion of the ossuaries **and** the photo presented had removed the three skulls by air-brushing! Second critical moment!

The plot thickens in October, 2002 with the emergence of the "James ossuary," the third critical moment! This episode is well documented and does not require repeating here. In fairness it must be said that a few scholars and archaeological administrators refuse to accept its authenticity, for whatever theological or political motives.

I am quite confident that IAA: 80/509 is the ossuary of "James, son of Joseph, brother of Jesus" for these reasons:

(1) the measurements of the box are an exact match for Shimon Gibson's missing tenth ossuary;

(2) the script has been authenticated by leading linguistic scholars;

(3) the patina has been absolutely verified as coming from the Talpiot tomb and matching that of the other nine ossuaries.

In 2005 James Tabor and Simcha Jacobovici "rediscovered" the Talpiot tomb, entering it on December 5. Their work is documented in a riveting program entitled "The Jesus Family Tomb" done by the Discovery Channel. Their work and interviews with IAA authorities uncovered only the nine ossuaries listed in the official catalogue and acknowledged by Amos Kloner. The IAA adamantly denied any possibility that the bones and ossuary of Jesus of Nazareth had been found.

You make up your own mind:

(1) IAA: 80/500

Mariamenon Mara: Master Mary"

This is the name and form for Mary Magdalene found in Epiphanus, Origen, the Pistis Sophia, and the Acts of Philip.

(2) IAA: 80/501

Yehuda bar Yeshua: Jude, son of Jesus

(3) IAA: 80/502

Matya: Matthew

(4) IAA: 80/503

Yeshua bar Yehosef: Jesus, son of Joseph

Mitochondrial DNA of 500 and 503 was analyzed and cross-referenced. These two individuals were **not** siblings, did not have the same mother.

(5) IAA: 80/504

Yosa: Joses of Mark 6:3

This is a very unique form of Joseph.

(6) IAA: 80/505

Maria: Mary

This form is unique but with precedence for Jesus' mother

(7) IAA: 80/506

No name

It has a X on one side.

(8) IAA: 80/507

No name

(9) IAA: 80/508

No name

(10) IAA: 80/509

Ya'aqob bar Yosef ahwi Yeshua: James, son of Joseph, brother of Jesus

* * *

Conclusion

Jesus of Nazareth was a first century CE rural Galilean, spirit-filled, wonder working, Davidic descendent, apocalyptic, itinerant preacher. He was born in Nazareth between 6-4 BCE, probably married to Mary Magdalene with at least one child, and crucified by Roman authorities on Nisan 15, 29 CE for sedition. His message was a radical call to enter the kingdom of God **NOW** by living an unselfish life of love in service to others. That message was misunderstood by Roman overlords and Jewish authorities and continues to challenge hearers today.

18166504R00084

Made in the USA
Charleston, SC
20 March 2013